FRACTAL

A Tale of Three Interventions

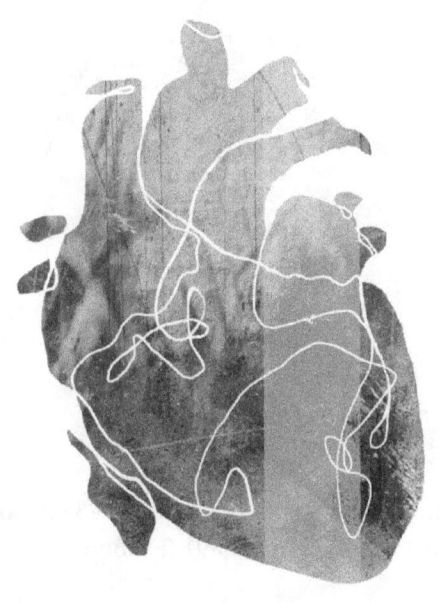

HELMUT MEIJER

For my dad,
Pieter Martinus Reid Meijer
(1938 - 2015)

whose heart I could never figure out.

"Fractal," by Helmut Meijer. ISBN 978-1-951985-89-9 (softcover); 978-1-951985-90-5 (hardcover); 978-1-951985-91-2 (eBook).

Published 2021 by Virtualbookworm.com Publishing Inc., P.O. Box 9949, College Station, TX 77842, US. ©2021, Helmut Meijer.

All rights reserved. No part of this publication may be reproduced, stored in a retrieval system, or transmitted in any form or by any means, electronic, mechanical, recording or otherwise, without the prior written permission of Helmut Meijer.

*"I am forgotten,
like one dead from the heart.
I am a vessel
that has lost myself..."*

- Ps 31:12

TABLE OF CONTENTS

PROLOGUE 1

BUT SHE WAS NAKED 3

TWO ROADS 15

FRAIL 33

SEMANTICS 59

SPACE BETWEEN 71

SEVEN 95

FALL OF ROME 119

STRONG 135

GAZE 147

HARD TO HEART 159

MAMMON 167

EPILOGUE 187

GLOSSARY 191

ACKNOWLEDGEMENTS 203

PROLOGUE

The journey that actuated the writing of this book, was and remains, arduous.

I do not believe that my own story is important enough – let alone that interesting – for *another* biography; rather, I feel compelled to share what I am discovering, as this may be of vital efficacy to many.

As I'm writing this, I am overtly aware of my heart and physically in discomfort. And I wish that this wasn't the case, as life was more facile prior to this awareness.

When it comes to the 'heart', countless songs, poems and books have been written on the subject. Yet society deals with matters of the heart in a universally insubstantial fashion. We casually equate the heart with love. And regardless of culture, language and ethnicity, we recognise the heart as central to our lives.

The heart has become synonymous with a myriad of our emotions, convictions and connections – and even our disconnect – to the material world and our human relationships. Yet rarely do we engage with the heart substantially – that is to say factually.

Over the past four years, I have had three coronary angiograms. For the nescient like myself, an angiogram is quite an invasive medical procedure that uses X-ray imaging to scan for restrictions in the blood flow going to the heart. As part of the intricacy of this procedure, clogged arteries can be opened through metal stent placement and/or balloon angioplasty.

Although the last of these three interventions triggered the conviction to write a book, the story I'm about to tell is, on the one end, about the journey of discovery of the sheer eminence of the heart, and on the other end about my personal unearthing of the Ancient Hebrew language. Where these two inimitable paths intersect is where we take off.

My prayer is that this book will help you connect with your own story, even as I share mine.

Here we go…

Helmut Meijer
Stellenbosch, August 2019

1

BUT SHE WAS NAKED

"lev tahor bara' li elohim…"

- Ps 51:10

The night is unusually quiet and clear. The air is inveigled with autumn as the months of dry, desert swelter lazily turns into cooler evenings.

Slowly but surely the season of festivities is drawing near.

As is the custom during this time of the year, the fighting men had left the city, and are now in the open fields, warring brutally against neighbouring *Ammon*. But for obscure reasons, the ruddy shepherd-boy-turned-king is not in the field.

David, unable to slumber, rises and walks out onto the roof of the palace overlooking the walled and flourishing citadel - now named after him. Rigged high up on the slopes between the *Kidron* and *Hinnom* valleys, the city of Jerusalem is safe and the people asleep.

David, glancing over the roofs below, notices what looks like a stranger bathing in the moonlight. There is a moment of hesitation. He traces the lustre of her glistening skin until terror and desire collide. She is *so* beautiful.

"Turn around, David. Now!" says the voice inside, but the visceral conquers resistance.

Vindicated by his impetus, the king investigates and has the stranger summoned to his quarters: a young woman whom his servants identify as *Bathsheva*, the daughter of an Israeli man, *Eli'am*, and wife of one of his own fighting men, *Uriyah*... a non-Hebrew.

The young Bathsheva spends a night with David, falls pregnant and has the king informed, who then realises that astute intervention is needed to masquerade their liaison considering that her husband is still on the battlefront.

David has Uriyah summoned back to the city in the hope that he would sleep with Bathsheva, for every obvious reason. But scripted irony: Uriyah refuses to be with his wife while his brothers and commander are encamped in the open field. And what began as a sleepless night for the king, now turns into orchestrated homicide.

A second failed attempt to lure Uriyah to be with his wife follows, and David sends him back to war, this time with clear instruction to *Yo'av* his commander to station him on the frontline, where the battle was fierce and sure to claim his life.

Following her period of mourning, David proceeds to marry the widowed Bathsheva. During this time, the trusted prophet *Natan* visits David who relates a story to him: A rich man heartlessly took from a poor man his only little ewe lamb - one that he bought and raised and whom his children loved - and dressed it for a random traveller who stayed over at the rich man's house. The story flares up David's anger, only for Natan to point out: "You are that man."

This sorrowful chapter in David's life concludes with the death of their newborn; an event that sheds much light on David's emotional wiring.

This is but a reductionist paraphrase of the tragedy captured in 2 Samuel 11 and 12. Rabbi's and Sages over the ages have debated whether the story of David and Bathsheva was really about lust. Or whether it actually articulates David's struggle with power, considering his contrived murder of Uriyah, the Hittite. Or even whether Bathsheva was *in* on the seduction from the beginning, seeing that her bathing on the roof was a ritual cleansing act after her menstrual period. She was most amenable to fall pregnant.

The text, however, is ambiguous about this. But whatever the case, this chapter in David's life highlights an all-pervasive reality… that David's story is our story.

Psalm 51 was written in the aftermath of David's ordeal with his now-wife Bathsheva and her late-husband Uriyah. Compelled by conviction, David begs YHWH to create in him a *clean heart* (Psalm 51:10). For many of us, this is probably one of the most quoted verses in our own wrestle with 'good and evil'.

But to have enough understanding about this significant petition of David, we would need to unpack some ancient concepts. Let's head back to the desert.

HEBREW

As part of the West Semitic branch of the Afroasiatic languages, Ancient Hebrew is a uniquely syncretised language, drawing from the influence and contribution of a number of desert-dwelling people groups.

Dating back to around the 10th century BCE (which incidentally frames the time during which David reigned), the Ancient Hebrew language employs what scholars call a *Paleo-Hebrew* alphabet. This variant of the Phoenician alphabet consists of 22 picture letters, each depicting a concrete concept understood within the nomadic culture.

Ancient Hebrew is a root-based, consonant-only language, which means that two or more pictures combined form fundamental building blocks (called 'roots') for both vocabulary (words) and syntax (language rules).

The Hebrew language is verb-based, where "action and function" take precedent over "form and appearance". Where our languages are all about outward appearances, the Hebrew language centres around actions.

Thus, our Indo-European (Latin-based) languages have almost nothing in common with Hebraic fundamentals: we are simply severed from almost everything that the Ancient Hebrew language and its accompanying worldview portray.

Our languages are mostly abstract and void of concrete association. We place a much stronger emphasis on subjects and objects over actions (verbs). That is why, when it comes to translating the Bible from Hebrew into any other language, the problem is quite simply... staggering.

LEV TAHOR BARA' LI ELOHIM

These are the transliterated words of David's famous prayer, "Create in me a clean heart, o God." Or literally translated, "[a] heart [that is] clean fashion for me Elohim."

The first thing to note is that David does not employ the verb "BARA" at the beginning of his plea. This is an exception for Biblical Hebrew. It only happens when the writer wants to draw specific attention to what comes before the verb. In this case: "LEV TAHOR" which informally translates to 'a [ceremonially] clean heart'.

Next up is the verb "BARA" followed by the phrase "LI ELOHIM" which informally translates to 'for me, [o] Elohim'.

In the light of Ancient Hebrew being a verb-based or action-oriented language, let's begin with "BARA".

This verb, used here in its simple form (also called the *pa'al* or *qal* form), occurs less than 50 times in the Biblical text. It's most often translated as "created", as in the famous opening verse of the Bible, "In the beginning, God *created...*" (Genesis 1:1)

But when one considers the various uses of "BARA", we end up with serious challenges.

For example, in 1 Samuel 2:29, the verb "BARA" is used in the context of fattening or filling up: "...*make yourselves fat* with the best of all the offerings..." In this case, the translation 'to create' would not bring across the point.

In Joshua 17:15 the same verb is used in the context of felling a tree: "…get thee up to the wood country, and *cut down* for thyself there in the land…" Again, 'to create' would not convey the right meaning.

So, what's going on here? From analysing the text as a whole, it seems that the verb "BARA" carries with it the idea of a process: something that needs time to materialise, almost as if the essence of the word refers to a transformation over time, from a simpler to a more complex state (rethink Genesis 1:1 from this perspective now.)

In essence, David is really asking God to begin a process in him, which involves change over time: to fashion in him something that will eventually render him in a state that is better or evolved.

Next, let's consider the subject of the sentence: "LI ELOHIM". This is fairly simple to translate, and can only mean 'for me, Elohim'. Before we look at the word "ELOHIM", something to note is that David does not ask God to 'fashion' something in him, but *for* him. It's nuanced, but it all adds up. At this point David acknowledges his need for an intervention - a work that solely lies with God.

The word "ELOHIM" is almost universally translated as 'God'. And this is a problem, since the word 'God' in English does not have a universal definition and consequently no universal application. The word "ELOHIM" is the Hebrew plural of the word "ELO'AH". And in turn the word "ELO'AH" has a short version "EL" which is used more in the Biblical text than the longer, more formal version. And here is where insight into the Paleo-Hebrew alphabet becomes essential.

The Hebrew word "EL" consists of two letters, and therefore two pictures: an "ALEPH" (picture of an ox) and a "LAMED" (picture of a shepherd's staff). The *aleph* or ox is understood to mean everything that the Ancients associated with this animal: servanthood, strength, patience, diligence. And the *lamed* or shepherd's staff is understood to mean everything associated with a shepherd: authority or leadership, protection, belonging, movement, journey. When these two pictures are combined, we get the idea of "an ox that leads" or "strong authority". This is quite far removed from our Western abstract idea of 'God'.

A second remark is that the plural form "ELOHIM" has a very specific use throughout the Biblical text. Hebrew plurals differ from Indo-European plurals in that plurality has more to do with repute than with number.

The concept of "ELOHIM" means "EL" in an exaggerated or plural state! This clarifies David's request. Before we move on to the Hebrew understanding of the heart, let us pause for a moment at the adjective "TAHOR".

In Hebrew an adjective occurs after a noun and takes on the properties (number and gender) of the noun it clarifies.

The adjective "TAHOR" is used to convey the meaning of 'undefiled' or 'unblemished' and ends up with two basic translations: *clean* and *pure*. In the case of vessels used in the temple, for example, the word 'pure' is undoubtedly the correct English word, and in cases where "TAHOR" refers to, for example, the condition of a body of water (see Leviticus 11:36), the apt English word would be 'clean'. Whichever the case, this adjective refers to an object in an undefiled state.

I find it interesting that most Bible translators decided on the word 'clean' for David's request from Elohim.

A final comment on "TAHOR" is that this adjective is derived from the verbal form "TAHER" which literally means 'to be bright' (luminous or radiant). A great example of this verbal form "TAHER" is found earlier in Psalm 51:7, "Purge me with hyssop and I shall be clean…" Literally, "…I shall be radiant…" This idea is beautifully embodied by the metaphor of a shining light.

Let's continue to the weightier matter of David's request and, in fact, the focal point of this book.

THE HEART

There are two related Ancient Hebrew words for 'heart': "LEV" and "LEVAV" with the latter being the longer variation of the first. Employing the beauty of the Paleo-Hebrew alphabet, the word "LEV" consists of two letters (two pictures): a "LAMED" (picture of a shepherd's staff, which we have discussed earlier) and a "BEIT" or "VEIT" (which has the picture of the floor plan of a tent). The letter *beit* has the literal meaning of a nomadic tent or a household, but also means 'inside' or 'within'. If we combine these two pictures, we get the Hebraic understanding of the heart: *authority within*.

Before turning back to David, let us take a closer look at this curious Hebraic idea of 'internal authority'.

The words "LEV" and "LEVAV" together occur more than 840 times in the Hebrew text, making it the most common anthropological term in the Bible.

The Ancients understood the heart to be the physical organ (capable of moving the rest of the body), but it was also understood to be the epicentre or the 'inner man' - in other words the mind and thoughts of man. This is important because in stark contrast with the Greco-Roman "body-soul-spirit" divide, the Hebrews understood 'the heart' to be exactly what the Greeks considered to be 'the soul'.

Incidentally - in Hebraic understanding - a living being consists merely of flesh ("BASAR") and spirit or breath ("RU'ACH").

A complete living being (flesh and breath) is considered a 'living soul' ("NEPHESH CHAYAH") in Hebrew. See Genesis 2:7.

Over and above this almost cardinal centre-of-a-being idea, the Ancients had other more esoteric associations with the heart, reflected for example in the use of 'heart' to mean 'inaccessibility' in Jonah 2:3: "You threw me into the depths, in the *heart of the seas."*

The list of alternative meanings (or alternative associations with the heart) is quite substantial and we will touch on some of these later.

Back to the 'authority within'.

This is the crux. And this where we rise and fall. This is where we begin to understand the habits we form and the patterns we live by, the constructive as well as the dark thoughts we entertain, the plans we make, the agreements we come to, the desires we succumb to, our hopes, our fears, our loopholes… everything!

Scripture makes some of the most evocative statements when it comes to the heart.

Jeremiah 17:9 calls the heart "deceitful above all things; and exceedingly corrupt". Proverbs 4:23 urges us 'to guard' our hearts from every side, because everything depends on it. Yeshua tells his followers in Matthew 5:8 that only those with *pure* hearts shall see God.

And the list goes on.

David, who asked of Elohim to fashion *for* him a pure heart, seemed to understand that at the core of his being, the 'authority' had become corrupted.

The very essence that governed his judgement - his ego - needed reconstruction. In fact, it needed replacement!

And David understood that this was going to require a process.

I believe we are invited to consider that the 'authority within' - until it is replaced with Elohim *Himself* - shall always be at war with Him:

the *only* Strong Authority.

2

TWO ROADS

"...I took the one less travelled by..."

- Robert Frost

"Whichever way they go, they're sure to miss something good on the other path."

- New York Times Sunday review on Fall of Frost (2008)

TRAIL

As is the case with every letter of the Hebrew alphabet, the letter "TSADE" - 18th of 22 consonants - reveals something important about the worldview of the ancient desert dwellers.

In the pre-exile script (often referred to as the *pictographic* script), the letter *tsade* had the picture of a trail or path with a definite split in the road.

This concept of a path with various turn-offs was fundamental in Hebraic understanding, since both the following of a prescribed path or the blazing of a new trail determined how the ancient nomads orientated their lives, and how they made decisions in austere circumstances. They understood that following a trusted or prescribed path (which would lead to water or pastureland), could save and preserve the clan; straying from it, could mean death.

Several Hebrew words reflect this. For example, the word "TSEDEK" translates to 'righteousness' in English. At best this translation conveys a religious or pious idea, and possibly because it is loaded with a lot of cultural subtexts. But most of the original meaning is probably missed because it rarely gets unpacked.

"TSEDEK" is spelled with three Hebrew consonants of which the first is a *tsade*. And like we've mentioned, a *tsade* has the picture of a trail or a path. This is followed by a

"DALET" and a "QUF", and these two depict the picture of a door (or entrance), and of light gathering on the horizon respectively. The ancient nomads would have heard three ideas reflected in the word "TSEDEK" - *path, door* and *gathering*. And these combined would probably have meant something like 'the path leading to the entrance of a gathering'. Consider now Jesus' well-known statement in John 14:6:

"I AM the way…"

And in John 10:1-3,

*"Most certainly, I tell you,
one who does not enter by the door
into the sheepfold, but climbs up some other way,
the same is a thief and a robber.
But one who enters in by the door
is the shepherd of the sheep.
The gatekeeper opens the gate for him,
and the sheep listen to his voice.
He calls his own sheep by name and leads them out."*
(WEB)

and verses 7 and 9:

"Most certainly, I tell you, I am the sheep's door…"

"I am the door. If anyone enters in by Me, he will be saved, and will go in and go out, and will find pasture."

No wonder Jeremiah alludes to Him as "YHWH, our Righteousness." (Jeremiah 23:6, WEB) To summarise, the idea of being 'righteous' from a Hebraic understanding, means to *follow the path* that leads to the entrance where people gather or assemble.

The Jewish people still have a concept central to their faith, called the "HALACHA". Loosely translated *halacha* means '[the] walk'. For them it is the prescribed way of how to do life in its most intricate detail.

For the ancient nomads, survival meant following the *prescribed* path that would usher them to food, water and shelter. The idea of YHWH God giving instructions to His people makes so much more sense in this light than in our culture, where any form of prescription poses a threat to our so-called freedom.

Western Christianity simply does not celebrate rules and laws. Quite the opposite! These are viewed as restrictive to *our* freedom. For example, when one drives on a highway, and suddenly a speed sign pops up, we interpret it as attempting to inflict a restriction on our freedom to go at whatever speed we choose (read: desire)!

In the ancient world, this metaphor of following a prescribed path was the knife's edge between life and death.

> *"Behold, I have set before you this day*
> *life and prosperity, and death and evil.*
> *For I command you this day to love Yahweh your*
> *God, to walk in His ways, and to keep His*

*commandments, His statutes, and His ordinances,
that you may live and multiply,
and that Yahweh your God may bless you
in the Land where you go in to possess it.
But if your heart turns away, and you will not hear,
but are drawn away, and worship other gods,
and serve them;
I denounce to you this day, that you will surely perish."*

- Deut 30:15-18 (WEB)

Let's remember the *tsade*. Every step of the way is part of the trail. And every split in the road matters.

DIVERGENCE

I grew up in the Karoo in the 80s.
...in a *very* musical home.

Both my parents were music teachers and performing musicians earlier in their lives. Our house was one jolly and amiable music school - for almost the duration of my school days. My sister dipped her toes into classical music, but she was really more into 80's synth-pop, doing maths and watching *No Jacket Required* almost every night. I loved it.

I didn't want anything formal to do with music, apart from singing at a local wedding now and then, while my dad played the organ. I have fond memories of those days. But that was all there was to it. I was a schoolboy for whom outdoor sports trumped cultural interests. This would later cause quite some tension in my life.

My mother - who [still] is the more conservative and traditional of my parents – tried everything she could to lure me into learning the piano. In my opinion to no avail but she still vehemently contests this.

My late father was a church organist and improviser. He spent most of his time at home just doodling around on the piano, but with a dexterity that I could never *really* decode. I was always amused by my parents' different approaches to music although they fully respected their differences.

As a schoolboy, I never followed their musical lead until it was almost too late. A moment of truth came in my second last year of high school when I was invited to participate in a music concert in a far-away town, with a handful of music students from our school. My only role was to sing a duet with a girl in my class. But that night I witnessed how a lad *just* two years older than me, performed David Foster's "Winter Olympics" theme song on the piano, flawlessly.

That night something shifted. It wasn't merely the brilliant performance that struck me, nor the amazing experience hearing somebody just about my age play so ridiculously well... more so it was the terrible moment of clarity: I've been granted every opportunity to embrace music the way my friend did, but wasted it. On our way back in the school bus that night, I asked God for another chance with music …

MOUNTAINS

(I am writing this from Zermatt Youth Hostel, high up in the Swiss Alps, with a perfect clear sky view of the Matterhorn.)

My mother employed the promise of outdoor equipment to bribe me to participate in a couple of piano lessons in primary school. I remember receiving a very basic tent (and feeling very excited!) by scoring high marks for some music theory exam. But beyond that, I don't recall a lot of overlap between music and my strange love for the outdoors. My parents did not know what to do with my obsessive interest in adventure.

I joined the local hiking club when I was about 12 years old, as did two or three of my close friends. I recall our first ever hike: a rather easy 12 km stroll over the Outeniqua Mountains. The view as we traversed the summit ridge that morning, was amazing. But aside from the beautiful views, that morning I discovered that a significant part of my heart truly belonged in the mountains.

Over the course of the years that followed, I would often daydream about the mountains. As I grew older and stronger, my yearning for longer and more challenging adventures increased.

Through mountaineering I developed a deep sense of independence. Although most of our mountain excursions were undertaken under the supervision of the older folks from our hiking club, we gravitated more and more towards adventures of our own. And also, to higher and more remote places that the older people weren't interested in.

CONVERGENCE

1996 was my final year of high school. I was elected as head boy, but I was everything a typical head boy was not: I didn't participate in team sports and was branded as one of the strange kids who would hang out in the mountains over weekends. Plus, I was also quite outspoken about my Christian faith. Besides this, I was now spending all of my daily breaks doodling around on the piano in the school hall... definitely frowned upon by the big boys!

I recall a weekend trip to the Swartberg Mountains - our beautiful, local mountain range - with one or two friends. We were hiking back on a Sunday morning and took a coffee break on a ridge overlooking the vast Klein Karoo. And as was our custom, our small FM transistor radio made its appearance.

I was ill-prepared for what would happen to me that morning.

I remember the sound of crystal-clear piano notes cutting through the silence of our coffee break. I had never heard a piano sound like that. The single, reverberating notes felt like molten lava flowing through my senses as it blended with dreamy textures and a synthesised groove that simply made my heart leap. I could *not* get enough. The torrent of delight was simply over the top!

I would later learn that the song I heard on the radio that morning was the late Robert Miles' "Children" - a track that not only rose to unprecedented stardom but became the foundation for an enormous shift in the way electronic music was perceived henceforth.

Little did I realise at the time how a Robert Miles track could connect the dots in my own life. In that instant mountains and music became less asunder. I spent most of my final year of school discovering the haunting *gravitas* between these two previously unreconcilable interests.

My mother bought me my first ever *Korg* Music Workstation (a keyboard with which you can sequence together different musical layers or parts) on which I spent days and nights figuring out how to bring some of my new-born ideas to life. Suddenly many of the sounds that my sister introduced me to through her love of *pop* music, were now within reach. I was hooked.

I took a gap year after school and joined a small music team that travelled the country and worked with school kids. We danced, we performed, we inspired, and we spread the Gospel! Young, crazy and naïve, we probably did a lot of damage through our exaggerated self-assurance. But we made *lots* of music and performed to crowds big and small. I loved every minute of it. The one thing that slowly began to transpire that year, was a deep desire *and* conviction to release my own songs.

After my gap year, my folks persuaded me to study for a BSc degree at Stellenbosch University. I protested but finally agreed under the sole condition that my science degree would further my future adventures.

But the very first day I had to cut open a dead hare in a Zoology class I realised that biological science might have been the incorrect choice. Staying motivated was going to be hard work.

Early in my first year I joined the evening band of our Student Church as a piano player and back-up singer. It was weird not to be in the leading role, but I enjoyed it, nonetheless. My studies followed a pattern of going to class, running in the mountains, going on weekend adventures and making music at church.

My roommate at my residence returned from an event one night and told me he had passed on my details to a local band: they were looking for someone with keyboard skills to help them record a CD.

(Yep. There was a time when people recorded CD's.)

Since I was already spending most nights behind my music workstation programming dance grooves, he thought I'd be a suitable candidate. Little did he know how this introduction would lead to a split in the road ahead.

I received a phone call from Neil Büchner, the leader of *Merchant Seal.* Neil came to see me, and the rest is history.

We made a CD together and I eventually joined the band as a keyboard player and back-up singer.

Becoming part of the Merchant Seal clan felt like *the* one thing that gave meaning to my three years of undergraduate studies. We performed all over campus and even in the greater Western Cape. Our band room in the basement of the theological school turned out to become our almost cultish hang-out place. I remember living in this basement room during several holidays, sleeping between musical instruments and camping gear.

Merchant Seal enjoyed favour across the various church denominations on campus, but curiously also in non-Christian circles. It not only had an important role to play in town, but the band also contributed greatly to my own sense of belonging. To this day many of my best friends were either part of the band, or part of the social life surrounding it.

Those days were amazing. We had a simple message encouraging our peers to turn to God. We made music that we loved. And we were family.

INTERVENTION

I had no idea what to do after my undergraduate studies. The one option was to continue with science, but I just couldn't see myself in a lab.

During my three years on campus I managed to sneak into the Conservatorium of our campus, almost daily. Initially it was frowned upon, but eventually the staff accepted me as one of the music students.

Towards the end of my third year, I enquired about the possibility of becoming more involved at the Conservatorium in any way. I just wanted to make music.

One of the Professors had heard about my unusual story with music. She also knew that both my folks were full-time musicians. She then told me about a brand-new postgraduate programme and that they were particularly interested in candidates who didn't follow a formal music education route. And voila! I was invited to enrol for a first of its kind *Master of Philosophy* in Music Technology.

Six students who were strangers to each other constituted the first intake of the programme. We had access to newly sponsored computer equipment worth hundreds of thousands of Rands. The existing facilities of the Conservatorium were archaic: tape machines, analogue recording desks, old speakers and vintage microphones. But rooms with world-class acoustics.

My academic promoter offered me free rein in the studios, under one condition: I had to be ready to teach a course in music production. He told me that I was welcome to record whatever and whoever I wanted as long as I'd figure out how everything worked. Carte blanche. Boom!

I spent many days and nights, even weeks and months, decoding what felt like a newly discovered spaceship. So much so that much of what I know about recording today, I discovered during that first year of our Master's degree.

At the beginning of 2001, Merchant Seal decided to disband, calling an end to what felt like the core of my campus life. It was extremely surreal.

We decided that Merchant Seal was going to have one final concert for friends and family, and that we were going to record the performance and release the album as our last offering. The evening transformed the ending of our band into something truly significant.

That night, a new dream was born.

Inspired by the bliss of capturing our final performance, my good friend, Daniel Steenkamp (our band manager and trained theologian) and I decided to start a new record label under the name *Merchant Records*. As with every split in the road, the decision Daniel and I took to launch a label, was going to impact my life as an aspiring musician, more than anything else.

Daniel and I were both post-graduate students. We loved adventure and new ideas. We were the perfect fit for either great success or a very sad story. Or both…

Three years of Merchant Records shaped us in a very particular way. We signed the rather eccentric World Music group, *DNA Strings*, who rose to unprecedented local stardom and made both parties lots of money.

Neither Daniel nor I knew anything about the music business or stewarding our newly discovered resources. We worked incredibly hard. And we played equally hard. We recorded many bands and solo artists and released a list of successful and less successful records. But the two of us eventually spent much more than necessary to make a commercial success of our label.

I purchased an old Series 3 Land Rover from a German touring couple who I met in Namibia. I couldn't really afford rent and ended up living in the mountains in my old Rover for almost three months. I'd work in the Conservatorium studios or in our offices during the day, and then I'd drive out to the mountains to sleep under the stars. Those were carefree days when it was still safe to do so.

As an aspiring label, Merchant Records had a good reputation in Stellenbosch and even beyond. But we ran out of steam when we lost just about everything at the end of our second year. Many days Daniel and I would sit in our usual coffee shop, not knowing what to say to each other. The pressure was simply getting the best of us.

Ridden with financial woes, we pulled the plug on Merchant Records about three and a half years down the proverbial rabbit hole. A well-known South African gospel artist took over the label, but we retained the debt.

It took several more difficult years for both Daniel and me to walk away from it all… *free*.

I was tempted in those years to flee the country. It was possible thanks to my late father who left me the enormous gift of an EU Passport! But I decided to stay in Stellenbosch and face my demons. After miracle upon miracle, I slowly emerged from the debilitating pressure resulting from our failed label.

SOLO

I started my own boutique company, *Helmut Meijer Music* in 2005. One of my first clients was my friend Neil Büchner from Merchant Seal. We crafted his debut solo album, "Element", and won a national gospel music award for it. I not only remember the incredible musical satisfaction and encouragement this afforded me, but also how the award inspired me to finally cut my umbilical cord with the University and open a studio at home.

My humble little studio included a white *MacBook*, a sound card, *Pro Tools* software, a *Korg* keyboard and one decent microphone. And I remember how I had to max out two credit cards to make that a reality. My sense of freedom working from home over-shadowed these early warning signals!

At a birthday party of a friend, I met the opera singer and neurologist Etienne van der Walt. He wanted to record his debut album and was scouting for the right outlet. We ended up listening to 80's music in his car, and the dream of making his album together was born.

I remember the morning that Etienne pulled up in front of my house in Stellenbosch. We brewed coffee, had a laugh, and started listening to music. It took us several weeks to record 12 songs, some of which I composed, but his album consisted mostly of a repertoire of his favourite 80's and 90's hits reinterpreted.

During this time *The Aeon Project* was born which comprised of Etienne, the peerless voice called *Nina du Plessis* and me. The three of us recorded an album called "Of Love and Life" that not only turned out to be the first South African album mastered at London's Abbey Road Studios, but more importantly gave birth to life-long friendships, and a shared journey of discovery called "music and the brain".

Those early days of working from home were blissful. I did some other small commercial projects and one of these earned me my first big radio hit called "High on Life" performed by the sensational *Lara Frances*.

SOBRIETY

I was almost fully booked for the year to come towards the end of 2007. That December I left for a three-week adventure holiday in South America.

I was joined by Dawie Verwey, one of my good friends and photographer for a local travel magazine. We cycled, swam in lakes, climbed a volcano, hiked the popular *Torres del Paine* route in Patagonia, dined, wined and simply had a fantastic holiday. All thanks to my life having normalised into something predictable: there was enough work, there was enough adventure. All was well.

On our way back to South Africa I received an email from my sister. She kept an eye on my diary while I was away. She told me that *every* single one of my bookings for 2008 had been cancelled. I was completely taken by surprise.

Taking off from the small airport at Punta Arenas, I scribbled in my journal that I had no idea what awaited me at home. Everything I thought was under control, everything that spelled complacency had collapsed in a single email. And the only thing I hoped for on that flight home, was that the God I was trying to follow, was still in control.

I do remember jotting down two things, both of which turned out to be essentially true: everything I have ever known was going to change. And *that* change was going to happen speedily.

3

FRAIL

*"A rose could never lie
About the love it brings
And I could never promise
To be any of those things."*

- Jars of Clay

This chapter was born in a mountain cabin,
high up in my childhood mountains.

MAN AND WOMAN

Much has been lost from the Hebrew translation of the story of Adam and Eve. Delving into the original meaning changes everything.

Adam's name is derived from the Hebrew word "ADAMAH" which means 'ground'. So, Adam is no superhero - he is from the dust of the earth! He is the main character for a short stint of the drama. In fact, we could view him as performing but a pre-show. Just kidding!

In the Creation narrative, Adam is 'fearfully and wonderfully made' (Psalm 139:14) - 'in the image' of his maker, YHWH Elohim (Genesis 1:26).

He is then appointed over every other living creature - to name them, subdue them, to till the ground... basically, Adam is made head steward over YHWH's creation.

But curiously, only until there is a counterpart for him does the concept of *male* and *female* surface.

YHWH Himself notes that it's not good for Adam to be alone. The Hebrew phrase "LO TOV HE'YOT HA'ADAM L'VADO" is translated as "[it is] not good for the man to be alone". But this particular phrase in Hebrew actually means, 'the man is not functional'. In other words, he lacks purpose on his own.

We all know the fascinating intervention that follows. YHWH tells Adam that He will make something *for* him. The Hebrew phrase "EZER K'NEGDO" is usually translated as 'helper' or 'suitable helper' or even 'a helper as his counterpart'.

While the word "EZER" certainly means 'helper', the word "K'NEGDO" is trickier. The root verb of "K'NEGDO" is the verb "NAGAD" which means 'to stand up against, to confront, to oppose'.

The prefix "K-" means 'like' and the suffix "-DO" is the possessive pronoun 'his' or 'for him'. Put together, "EZER K'NEGDO" sounds something like, 'a helper like one that will oppose him' or 'a helper like his opposition'. Imagine that! In short, we are dealing with a military phrase. YHWH tells Adam that He will make Him something without which Adam has no fighting chance.

A final remark on *ezer k'negdo* is that the idiom can be understood as follows: Adam's helper will be a blessing when he does what is right, *but* she will stand up against him when he does what is wrong.

The word 'Eve' is the translation of the Hebrew word "CHAVAH" which means 'life-giver'. I find it interesting that the word 'Eve' made it into our translations - it simply doesn't occur anywhere!

The first time we hear of man and woman (husband and wife), and male and female comes up next. The Hebrew word for man, when used in conjunction with his counterpart, is the word "ISH" and the word for female is

"ISHAH" - respectively 'man, husband' and 'woman, wife'. Curiously, before YHWH made the woman, the word for man was simply: Adam. The sages suggest that without a woman, man is simply Adam - from the ground. Some even suggest that unless a man is married, he is but a boy! Inconvenient, but fascinating.

The Hebrew word "ZAKAR" which is translated as 'male', literally means 'to remember'. The Hebrew word "NEQEVAH", which is translated as 'female', needs a little more explanation. The root verb of "NEQEVAH" is "NAQAV", meaning 'to pierce'. Quite loaded with sexual innuendo, "NEQEVAH" means 'the *one* that is pierced'. But this powerful idiom in Hebrew goes further. While the man pierces the woman, in Hebrew the 'pierced one' is the one that surrounds and protects: [she is] the boundary-setter.

This is where we might miss the functional delineation of man and woman in our Western understanding. YWHW charges the man - Adam - with only one thing: to remember Him. And the woman - the female - He charges with another: to surround and protect Adam.

What does this mean in practical terms? Western culture has demoted both man and woman to fit our small-minded social norms, but in Hebrew God expects a man to listen and remember His words. And He expects a woman to take whatever actions needed to ensure that Adam is always listening and doing what God has said. In a way, she is granted the power of attorney to correct his course of action.

I have witnessed *so* many people come to liberty in their marriages, and I've witnessed so much amazing fruit that this bears in many lives - yet, ironically, I lived with this truth amid my own struggle. And I did not win the battle of my heart.

DECEPTION

Genesis 3:1 relates that 'the serpent was more subtle than *any* animal of the field that YHWH had made'. The Hebrew word "ARUM" is behind the translation of the word 'subtle'. It means 'crafty, shrewd, sly, cunning'.

Now… watch what happens. In the narrative, the serpent does *not* check on Adam regarding fruit and diet. He goes to *Chavah* whose purpose or function is to protect Adam. And he checks with her if she remembers what YHWH had said to them. As a reminder, apart from all the normal trees, YHWH specifically mentions two trees: one was the Tree of Knowledge of Good and Evil (in Hebrew, the discernment between 'functionality' and 'straying from the path'). And the other tree was the Tree of Life, "in the middle of the garden."

Take note of the old serpent: He asks Chavah to account for what God has said.

But that was Adam's function. *Her* role is to make sure Adam is positioned correctly. So, one possible reading of this might be that her assessment of the situation was that if they would eat from the Tree of Knowledge of Good and Evil, she would be able to better protect and steer him. Maybe. The text is ambiguous on this.

But one thing we know for sure: when Chavah offers Adam the fruit, he does *not* remember the words of Elohim at all.

He happily obliges.

We could argue that the way Chavah interpreted the situation means she may simply have been misled, but Adam, quite frankly, did not remember. This was his sole assignment in this functional unity of theirs. The words Adam did *not* remember are quite striking: "... in the day you eat of it, you will surely die."

The next chain of events follows a sad and predictable pattern: realisation, and then trying to cover up things. Scripture relates that they 'heard the voice of YHWH God walking in the Garden," (Genesis 3:8) but they hid themselves.

In the next scene, YHWH Elohim, Adam, Chavah and the serpent are together. YHWH continues to pronounce the sentence (read: consequence) of their decision to trust themselves more than Him. He also announces the serpent's end as an eschatological sentence: the eternal victory of the seed of Chavah comes through the future Messiah's victory over sin and death.

YHWH says to Chavah that her pain in childbirth would be increased greatly, but possibly also that she would have pain in 'raising' her kids.

Although this part could be either translated as birthing or raising, there *may* be something else here: an allusion to the impact of the mother-child dynamics on the relationship between Adam and Chavah. YHWH says there will now be a distortion in this relationship. She will now *desire* him. This is different to the original reason why she was made!

But even worse - and as a result of this - Adam will now rule over her. Perhaps this is because of the distrust Adam now has of Chavah's gift. The text is not clear. But the problem prevails in our relationships today.

The next sentence reads: "Because you have listened to your wife's voice..." (Genesis 3:17). Stop. This is very important. The point is NOT that Chavah had spoken. Or that Adam listened to his wife. The point here is Adam did NOT listen to God. He did NOT remember the words of YHWH. Which is essentially being male.

The text goes on to say: "...cursed is the ground for your sake." There is no simple explanation for this. YHWH tells Adam that from this day forward, his efforts - even all his right efforts - will have no guarantees of success (See Genesis 3:19). This is a very hard and true reality. Only after this did Adam name his wife *Chavah* - mother of all the living.

Adam and Chavah begin their journey. Adam, most probably distrusting of her ability (her God-given superpower to protect and steer him), now decides to do it on his own. He lords over her, rules her, and he misses the essence: he cannot survive without her direction.

Chavah is stuck with all the God-given power to help (even confront!) Adam that is henceforth geared (even diluted?) towards her children. A purpose for which this covenant power was *not* designed.

I realise this is hard to digest. We know what happens next. Adam and Eve beget Cain and Abel (Hebrew "QAYIN" and "HEVEL"). It is interesting that with everything taken into account, Cain murders Abel.

To summarise: God fashions for Adam a helper who has the God-given power - even anointing - to continuously steer and [re]direct him [back] to God. A miserable deception happens with dire consequences.

The woman - Adam's military aid - is now rendered vulnerable on a level that disempowers her to apply her gift. Adam in turn chooses to rule over her and to decide for himself. The woman, who has little choice left, redirects her God-given power… to her children.

And *this* is our story.

This is our *dilemma.*

MEET

December 1997.

During my gap year our music team helped facilitate a camp for final year high school students at a last event for the year. Our team was mainly responsible for the music.

We hung out with the kids and had loads of fun. I remember how we had a wonderful and innocent time.

Or did we...

I met a beautiful, introverted girl (let's call her Alina), and the two of us danced every night and had fabulous chats over a few days. The last evening, however, Alina was missing in action, and after searching for her everywhere, I found her in her room. She sternly confronted me about whether it was my style to treat girls with all forms of charm and then just walk away? I was taken aback. Mainly because I had no dating experience. Sombre story short, we parted ways.

During my second year at varsity, I returned from a jog one afternoon and bumped into two students relaxing on the lush green lawn in front of their female residence. The one girl and I had become friends through playing together in the church band, and the other was going to become my friend.

We had a quick banter, and I left *fascinated*.

Many months went by and one day out of the blue I received a phone call from Michaela (this is not her real name). She had heard via the grapevine that a group of our friends was going to climb Kilimanjaro the following year.

And she got onboard. I was fascinated again.

We were a group of 16 strong-willed personalities who were to climb Kilimanjaro and make it down again in 6 days and visit Zanzibar afterwards. Michaela and I had minimal interaction leading up to our departure for the two-week journey.

It was in Zanzibar that I first experienced a kind of internal short-circuit. I recall one warm evening on the beach - calm ocean, palm trees, music playing from the beach bar, everyone dancing in the humid moonlight - that I truly noticed Michaela.

And with that came a palpable shift.

During the next couple of years, many of my friends fell in love with her. Many were utterly *convinced* that Michaela was their wife.

Meanwhile, Michaela and I were becoming really good friends. I vowed inwardly to protect this woman and kept this formidable stance that I would simply safeguard her. As months and years went by, we built trust and discovered shared humour. I still did not understand my fascination with Michaela, given that she had confided in me about her own struggles.

Michaela and I developed our own, private language, calling each other by *noms de plume*. And we regularly bantered about getting married if we'd both still be single when I would turn 30.

In my fourth year at varsity, I received an email from a girl with an email extension "@skydivesessex.com". Yes please!

It was Alina, of course. Yet now it was four years down the line. I had completed my undergraduate studies, and she was a skydiver in the States. I loved it. Within a rather short period of time, our to-and-fro emails became a daily rhythm. I was studying for my Masters, but I recall my days centred around hearing back from her. Long story short, I slowly but surely fell for Alina (or at least the idea of her).

On the same day of the Twin Towers' saga in 2001, she went missing from communication for days. The silence affected me in a way that was quite indicative. After a series of spirited phone calls, I tracked her down in Fort Lauderdale in Florida. We spoke and I decided that I was going to fly to the US to meet her in the months to come. I was convinced that all of this was turning into a fairy tale!

I was booked as a keyboard player for South African gospel singer *Louis Brittz'* UK tour and everything worked out for me to fly to Miami with the cash I made during the tour. However, Alina informed me that she started seeing someone…

I arrived in Miami, not even sure how Alina looked anymore (those were the days before social media), and there was also this nagging reality that there was another man in the picture, although that didn't break my speed.

Pressing through the multitudes on arrival at Miami Airport, Alina stood waiting for me - dramatic as from a movie scene. She ushered me to the commune where she lived with eleven muscular men all working on the yachts. I was slightly intimidated. But assured of my mission: Alina was going to become my wife.

We took a weeklong road trip, cruising through several states and camping out under the stars wherever we reached that day. We enjoyed coffee and wine, rowed on lakes, cooked food on campfires, and had the most incredible week together. In my mind, the deal was done.

But the last evening she dropped the bomb: "You're everything that I want in a man. But I am in love with somebody else." I didn't sleep at all that night.

The following morning Alina took me back to Miami Airport. We exchanged letters and gifts. I was instructed not to open her letter until high in the sky. Which I did. And in the letter, she prompted me to meet her in *Jongensfontein* (a small village on the south coast) on the 13th of December that year. All of my hope flared up.

I arrived in Jongensfontein, spirited and on time. But Alina was nowhere. My heart was racing. I searched for her and eventually made my way to her parents' homestead nearby. Her mom casually informed me that she never came home and was on holiday with her boyfriend in the Canadian Rockies. I was flabbergasted. After relaying my disappointment by email, she replied nonchalantly that she could *hear* I was disappointed and asked me to come *again* to Jongensfontein in March the following year.

My hope wasn't completely dashed. I returned to meet Alina. But she never came. Shortly after this I read in a blog entry of a close friend of mine that Alina got engaged.

TURNING OVER

In 2007 - I was 29 at the time - Michaela joined me and a group of friends on a cycle tour adventure in Namibia. Over the course of two weeks, she and I had amazing interaction - at least in my mind. I confronted the awkward situation of there being 'one year left before I turn thirty'. She seemed quite perky about it. We returned to South Africa. But my existing confusion about our situation became one level deeper.

After the credit crunch hit in 2007, I packed up my life early the next year and left South Africa with the hope of settling in the UK.

I stayed with my doctor friend Nellis van Zyl Smit (who was the lead singer of our late campus band, *Merchant Seal*) and his violinist-turned-chartered-accountant wife, Helene (the lady who was present on the day that I met Michaela).

For my birthday weekend I went to Scotland with some close friends. Everyone there was reasonably informed about *my* inner vow of getting married at 30. And although this was nothing short of outlandish, my friends offered their best support.

Following what felt like the longest and strangest phone call to her parents, from the summit of Scotland's *Ben Nevis*, I cold-called Michaela in South Africa. I was shaking with total hesitation and unrivalled excitement: I proposed over the phone.

And from what I remember *that* phone call really caught her … off-guard. "I can hear you are serious, Helmut. I cannot answer you right now. But can you meet me in Switzerland in four days?" were her words in her silky but controlled tone of voice. We hung up.

That was a moment of truth: I was fully caught up in a one-sided deal.

At that point my fascination with Michaela had already totalled nine years of my adult life.

Very few people knew about the unceremonious way in which my castle in the sky collapsed in the 24 hours that followed. Michaela pointed out over the phone the next day that she would need to "think through this a thousand times". I was confused, to say the least. I responded, "I will call you when I am over you."

Seven months passed. On a cold November morning in the town of Leeds, North-England I recall my sense of freedom: I *was* over her.

Finally.

In the bluster of the moment, I emailed her. I wanted to see her so we could talk through everything. She emailed me back almost immediately, and within minutes we had a date confirmed for that December when I would visit my family in South Africa.

We met in Pretoria at a restaurant. We were the only people there that night. After a bottle of wine and four hours of tug-and-pull later, we got up from the table to head our separate ways. As I rose from the table that evening with a sense of clarity, wrapping up almost a decade of fascination with this woman

We hugged sincerely. And we kissed goodbye. But we lingered. And the kiss that was supposed to be a friendly parting, at *that* moment, made finality swivel into a question.

I went back to South Africa on the 29th of April 2009, almost twelve months later to the day since my arrival in the UK. I would later learn that those twelve months depicted a Hebrew sabbatical year called the *Shmitah.*

Life returned to normal. I fell back into composing and producing music.

On my birthday the next year, exactly one year after my proposal to Michaela, I received a phone call from her. We bantered for what felt like an hour, and she told me in passing that she was on her way back to South Africa. Friends and I planned to visit the Cederberg Mountains, and it was quickly decided that Michaela would join us.

I remember the July afternoon she walked nonchalantly into my house in Stellenbosch as if nothing ever happened. We headed off to the Cederberg. We spoke about life, about the past years both living abroad, about Israel... About two hours into our drive as we were crawling up the Gydo Pass outside Ceres, I sensed that she seriously wanted to speak to me about something.

"About the fact that you proposed to me last year," I listened intently. "I think I made a mistake; I think I *may be* your wife."

Silence.

A thousand thoughts veered through my mind. Between the two of us, Michaela is the introvert, but I was without words. I remember merely feeling strangely relieved. As if more than a decade came full circle. I asked her what she expected me to do with this information. "Nothing," she replied. "I just think you should know."

And we drove into the night.

WHAT IF

Our weekend in the Cederberg was charged. Even magical. We were very aware of each other. And just about everyone could pick up on *that*. I remember my continuous sense of a 'full circle'. Not even knowing what it meant.

Michaela had to leave a day earlier than the rest, and as we greeted at her car, we kissed goodbye. And lingered again. Those who saw us later asked me what was going on. In my mind, I felt nothing but relief.

The Monday evening after our weekend in the mountains Michaela came to stay over at my place. And in the apparent aftermath of a persuasive conversation she had with a friend, that evening we kissed. And we kissed well. It was ten years down the line. To this day I remember the picture I saw in my mind's eye: a bent frame being pulled right.

Michaela left for Pretoria the following day, but the text messages we exchanged were different. Something serious had happened between us. About ten days later, Michaela came back to Stellenbosch. This time we were going on a road trip to her friends in the Eastern Cape. We left, for the first time in a state of mutual togetherness that neither of us had experience in.

Those nine days of travelling together were filled with such solidarity that had they been the only time we were ever going to have together; they would have been enough. We decided - to finally give our 'relationship' a chance.

On our way back from the Eastern Cape Michaela told me that she had accepted a vocation with the United Nations in North Africa starting within a month. And it was going to be for a year at least. I was dumbstruck. What was more, she was about to leave on a three-week holiday to Europe with friends. And I was not invited.

We had little communication during her trip to Europe. There was one night though... I was encamped out in the mountains with some of my friends, and I tried to connect with Michaela. There was some sort of response. But I recall falling seriously ill that night, on a deep heart-level.

Michaela worked and lived together with a group of ex-pats in harsh circumstances. And this was our strange relationship: conversing daily for a few minutes via Skype. I went to bed most nights, tensed up with angst and frustration. She was my dream come true, but this was not the life I imagined. My heart suffered immensely. And very few people knew.

We made plans to meet up in Egypt that November. It made sense from Michaela's leave-perspective and from my unsatiated desire for another adventure. I flew to Cairo and waited at the airport for her flight from Sudan. It was a near-surreal scene when we united again after so many months of internet communication. And like high school lovers we headed off to Sinai by bus.

I think we had only 4 days together. We both fell ill on the second day. Michaela got better; I got worst. And in the awkwardness of me being really sick for the remainder of the time, I felt that there was something else lurking beneath the surface. I had my suspicions. Matters deteriorated seriously between us. I sat at the window seat of my aeroplane that night with her flight to Sudan parked right next to mine. We were about to depart in different directions.

Movie scene. Dream woman. Cataclysmic abyss between us. I was really ill.

Back in South Africa, I was diagnosed with a stomach ulcer. "Stress," was the doctor's verdict. It was less than a month to Michaela's 30th birthday. I was put on strong medication for the ulcer. But suffice to say that those 30 days leading up to her birthday were rough. We had minimal communication. And I was not getting better.

The arrangement we had was that after her birthday celebrations we would spend some time with family and then spend a few days together around and after New Year's.

Michaela's 30th birthday (my late father and she were born on the same date) was held at a wedding venue in the mountains outside the Garden Route town of George. It was a beautiful event, decorated with toasts, dining and dancing. There was only one problem that night: her heart was not with me.

I wrote a song for Michaela's birthday called 'Turning Over'. The song was crafted to give voice to her complex life working for the United Nations under severe social and political pressure. I remember searching for words to frame her reality, only to discover later that the entire narrative of the song turned out to be our story - "I traded all my pearls for this burn."

Driving back to the cottage Michaela's family had rented - I played her birthday song. For me, at least, it was overwhelmingly gripping and symbolic.

We arrived at the cottage after midnight and she asked me if I'd mind sleeping outside. The cottage had only one double bed, and she was going to share it with her friend.

As I was lying outside, I texted her to come out so we could talk. Fifteen minutes of silence. "Let's speak in the morning. Now is not wise." was the last I heard from her that night.

I didn't close an eye and got up at 5 am to draft an email in which I pulled the plugs on us. I was devastated yet determined. Truthfully, after 11 years of this kind of self-betrayal, there was not much left of me. Then there was a knock on my car window *just* before I pressed "send".

I got out, and I lost my cool for the first time I can recall. Between my uncontrolled outburst and the subsequent release, there was a sincere embrace. Holding her intensely always felt very real.

I left and went to my parents' home later that morning. We didn't really speak for 4 days.

On the 31st of December I left the Karoo for New Year's Eve in Hermanus. I texted her to hear how she was. And where she was spending the evening. "Hermanus." Maybe

God was in this after all. We said that we might see each other that night. It was after-all… New Years. At around 23:30 I tried to phone her. Several times. No answer. I took the road just before midnight, in search of her.

Nothing.

I went to bed at 2 am that morning - not a word or trace of her.

On that peculiar morning of the 1st of January 2010, Etienne, one of my best friends who deeply understood my journey with Michaela, went with me to one of the beaches. I had another night of zero sleep. With first light we brewed some coffee.

As we unpacked the dilemma of the night before, lo and behold… Michaela and her friends came running past us and headed for the water. They did not see us. We watched them - as in a dream - as they exuberantly enjoyed the New Year's morning in the crashing waves. About half an hour later, they headed back up the stairs and walked right into us. It was a moment I would rather not have had.

I arranged to pick up Michaela from a friend's place around lunch. Etienne's cousin who was a clinical psychologist stayed on the same premises as we did, and I had a chat with her prior to picking up Michaela.

I spent about three hours relating my story of Michaela. And I remember her tearing up: "I have never seen a young man as strong but as destroyed as you are." Her words cut right to the heart.

"You have only one option left. Walk away."

With these words I left to pick up Michaela. We headed off along the coast and had an almost seven-hour conversation. About everything. It was brutal, it was rational, it was healing. I remember one of the hardest lines ever, "You are not strong enough for me." And although I should have taken her back to her friend that night, we spent two more days together.

Our mutual and parting consent was that it was over. And that I would not be there for her when she returned to Sudan. I was torn.

Etienne waited for me at the pharmacy where he sorted me out with sleeping medication and stuff for anxiety. It really helped in the weeks that followed.

Some months later I noticed one morning that Michaela was online on Facebook Chat. I messaged her and she instantly disappeared. Moments later she texted me, "I need to know that you have no expectations of me."

We agreed to a phone call that afternoon. It was incredible to hear her voice for those 30 minutes. But she was stern and focussed. The bottom-line of our dialogue was that I admitted that I believed she was my wife. Whatever was the case, she disagreed. And we hung up.

The following day I left with friends for a 5-day Orange River adventure in the hope of fixing the pain. I was a mess. And as per usual, running off on an adventure merely bought time.

I kind of moved on with life, whatever this meant. Eight months passed. Michaela phoned me. She was house-sitting in Somerset West and wanted to see me. What I should have said was, "Thank you, but no." But I couldn't. I met her that night at the apartment where she stayed. Eight months were not enough: we passionately embraced and kissed each other.

A month of on-and-off seeing each other ended when she told me she was simply "not romantically into this". Since this story was taking on severely toxic measures, I suggested that we drive into the mountains and go pray about this, together. Which we did. She left for Pretoria the next day.

The patterns of destruction (at least for me) were more or less the same: see each other after months, try not to be physical, fail at it, kick up dust and confusion, and part ways.

We met for a dinner in 2013. I remember it as a constructive meeting. That evening I told her that I'd give 'us' one last chance. My sincere belief was that if she'd face her demons and choose us, I would take her and make her my wife. No questions asked.

Michaela and I had a pivotal Skype call in 2015, an hour-long dialogue during which she boldly pointed out that the fictitious version of her that I had been 'in love' with for so many years, may very well have been mostly an outcome of my imagination. That conversation let us both off the hook.

To be absolutely fair, this is but a rough sketch of our fateful journey of love that did not work out, and it is but *my* subjective account of a *broken* heart. A much more powerful read would be our respective versions placed alongside each other.

If it was contained in a shorter period of, say, a year or two, the outcome might have been very different. But this near-relentless chronicle of attraction - undoubtedly on very different levels for her - went on for almost 15 years of my adult life. The only reason why I share this story is that what happened to me years down line, makes complete sense against this backdrop.

My late father was an incredibly kind and understated man. Deeply introverted, mysterious and really intelligent. We got along well, although we'd sometimes not speak for months. But one thing is sure: I could never completely figure out his mind. And as much as I employed my best and natural strength to try and 'win him over' - I could never.

He passed away in 2015 and left this same overwhelming sense with me: that I could never break through to him.

I fell in love with Michaela for exactly this reason. She represented everything I could never conquer in my own father. Psychologists call this the *imago.*

Even though I have known this phenomenon for years I have learned that knowing something, even of this magnitude, is no guarantee for *anything* else.

At times the journey simply has to be taken - *all* the way.

4

SEMANTICS

"Move yourself
You always live your life,
Never thinking of the future

Prove yourself
You are the move you make

See yourself
You are the steps you take

You and you, and that's the only way
You're every move you make…
So the story goes

Owner of a lonely heart (much better than a)
Owner of a broken heart…"

- Yes

In 2008 the credit crunch hit the entire world. Those serving in the non-essential sectors were hit particularly hard. As a young music producer, I was one of them.

When I emigrated to London at the age of 29, I thought it was going to be an easy relocation and setting up of my small, freelance business in England, but as many people know, the thirties have a knack of making you grow up… fast.

My *new life* in England panned out to serve a very specific purpose, demarcated by a short, but specific period of time and the most significant turn-off on my path.

HOME FROM HOME

London was in no way a new place for me. I worked there for two holidays during my undergraduate years.

At the end of my first year, three friends and I jumped on the working-holiday-visa bandwagon. I arrived in a freezing London and ended up as a kind of truck driver meets removal-boy (which was really humbling although I became very fit and travelled through much of England).

The other working holiday came at the end of my third year, this time working on a farm, cutting and netting Christmas trees. Looking back now, *that* was a hilarious experience!

I spent three incredible weeks with my friend Wil Punt (who is now a sought-after photographer). I also discovered pipe-smoking that holiday. It has inspired many a legendary mountaineer, and to this day I can still relate.

This time around I arrived in London in April 2008 and headed straight to my friends Nellis and Helene's cosy flat in New Malden. We agreed that I would only stay a month at their place - a kind of halfway house - but it turned out to be an entire year. For those who have not lived in a two-bedroom apartment in England - it is not designed for three adults. But these two exceptional humans let me stay with them, zero questions asked. I can testify to the love and sacrifice of my two incredible friends who could discern the importance of what was *truly going on* in my life that year.

I needed a safe haven for what I was going to discover that year. Nellis and Helene provided that home, albeit at a really high cost.

SHABBAT

Before the 25th of April 2008, I had never heard of a *Shabbat* meal. Let alone experience one.

Nellis casually informed me that they had started celebrating the Shabbat, which entailed resting on Saturdays, but which began and centred around a Friday evening family meal where several rituals were observed.

I was curious.

A massive lamb shoulder made it onto the festive table, further decorated with candles, a strange braided bread, olive oil, wine and flowers. The evening began. Nellis explained the meaning of the evening as Helene lit the candles and Nellis poured wine to overflowing, broke the bread and said some prayers - some in a language I have never heard. A very interesting late-night followed.

It was amazing to finally be with friends with whom I had such a long connection, but the newness of this Shabbat evening didn't sit well with me. I felt like there was a divide between myself and the Van Zyl Smit's. But I also recall a serious sense of betrayal that night.

Why has no-one ever told me *anything* about something *so* intrinsic to the culture of the Bible? We went to bed that night after a long catch-up and discussion about Nellis and Helene's journey leading to their observance of Shabbat.

It took three more Friday evenings before a strange thing happened to me. By the fourth Shabbat meal, I felt less weird about it all, and I recall the moment when Nellis poured wine into the glass, letting it overflow into a saucer, and praying that God would overflow through us in the same way... that *something* in me shifted.

I didn't speak out about it immediately, but the following morning when the house was still quiet, I googled everything that I could think of on the subject... *Hebrew, Shabbat, Israel,* ...

I remember the scores of open tabs on the computer filled with bits and pieces that felt like a treasure-hunt pulling me in. Strange letters, pictures, books, websites... I was on a slippery slope of joy and terror and everything in between. I did *not* come to London looking for this, but in that instant, I knew that this was the beginning of a new path for me.

On that peculiar Shabbat morning in May 2008, my journey with an incredible, but very different language began.

The three of us shared countless Shabbat meals that year, we dug deep into everything we never had the chance or the courage to question or unravel. The Bible sprung to new life, even much more than in the days when I first began my journey with God.

CONTEXT

I applied for hundreds of jobs in London and the greater UK. This process went on for weeks. But nothing worked out, except for one interview at the British Academy of New Music - a Popular Music school affiliated with the University of Westminster, called "Access to Music".

The position was to teach a subject called "Applied Composition" which is the fancy term for film music.

Although my hopes and doubts were balanced the day of the interview, the panel's response was surprisingly positive! I landed the *only* job that I was going to do for my entire time in London.

I had to travel once a week, very far from New Malden in the South West to the Academy in the east of London, to teach for three hours. But the job helped me to contribute somewhat to our food and wine.

My teaching days were immensely inspiring and unwittingly fashioned in me a great love for film music. I had to read a lot because almost everything I taught was also new to me. Although my journey with Applied Composition was mostly theoretical, I can see now how it shaped my interest in writing music for multi-sensory disciplines.

Apart from my small teaching job, my days in London consisted of going for long runs, occasional visits to the local gym, helping with the household, going for long walks at night, but most of all: studying Hebrew.

Only when I returned to South Africa did I realise how much that year in London contributed to laying a solid foundation for my Hebrew studies.

As time went by, trickles of production work started rolling in from South Africa. I produced some singles and one or two albums for artists back home, but as my year came to an end, I experienced a strong pull to return to South Africa.

I had two items on my bucket list before flying back: climb *Jebel Toubkal* with Nellis, and visit Israel. The former was for adventure. The latter felt necessary.

MOROCCO

Nellis and I left for Morocco early in March 2009. And after a couple of days in Marrakech, we headed for the infamous Atlas Mountains to climb Jebel Toubkal (4,167m) - the highest peak in North Africa. In contrast to several first world mountaineering trips, visiting the Atlas Mountains included an encounter with Moroccan hospitality. We headed off on the Toubkal trail on a cold autumn morning, but we had hardly started before we found ourselves relaxed in a Moroccan village, sipping mint tea and having a hand-gesture conversation with the locals.

Unfortunately, Nellis fell ill with altitude sickness that night, and I ended up scrambling up Jebel Toubkal mostly solo. I almost froze to death on my way to the top. I joined two foreigners for the summit push and luckily made it back to the mountain hut before dark.

Nellis returned to London, and I stayed behind in Morocco for another week or so.

Inspired by a backpacking trip that my friend Wil Punt and his wife did years earlier, I decided to cross the High Atlas Mountains... solo.

On my way to the obscure *M'Goun* Massif, the taxi bus stopped at a small village called *Azilal*. Here I recorded a piece of the afternoon prayer broadcasted from the local minaret; a song called "Cry for Azilal" was born from this recording sometime later.

The bus dropped me off by the side of the road, somewhere close to another village called *Agouti*. I was overwhelmed by the size and splendour of the Central Atlas Mountains. I was also disoriented and had no real idea of where I was except for vague directions and an oblique description of the 4-day trail ahead.

After hiking down a very steep path into the *Bou Gomez* valley, I pitched my tent next to a large river. And apart from feeling truly alone and overwhelmed by the noise of the water, I also started experiencing the first symptoms of a cold that night. The prolonged exposure to sub-zero temperatures of the previous weekend's climb compounded my situation.

I decided to be brave and undertake the odd 70 km hike alone and with no cell phone reception! The allure of the mountains was calling me away from common sense.

By late afternoon, after walking for hours with a heavy pack, my body started to cave in. My cold was now getting serious! With my limited orienteering skills, I could deduce that the village I was hoping to reach had to be near. I rested for a bit and then saw an old man riding on a donkey, heading straight to where I was sitting in the sun.

He approached me with kindness and gestures offering to take my backpack on his feeble donkey. I think he could see I was *not* okay. At first my pride resisted, but I felt really sick. Loading my heavy alpine pack on his animal almost made the poor thing collapse.

I slowly followed the Moroccan man on his donkey for what felt like kilometres. We were unable to engage in any form of dialogue. We parted ways at a split in the road high above a vast wadi. I handed him some Dirhams (it felt like he needed them more than I did); and in that vulnerable moment I was confronted with what *had* to be: the heart of God.

For both of us.

Less than an hour later I stumbled into the quaint village of *Rougoult* and pitched my tent under a tree. A woman from the village came directly to me and from her reaction I could tell that she realised I was in trouble. She brought me some water and even gestured whether or not I was hungry.

That night I had trouble breathing. My tent was pitched near the snowline of the M'Goun Mountains - with no cell phone reception - and nobody knew where I was. That lonely night made me reconsider where I would draw the line going forward. What would happen if I'd die somewhere in the Atlas Mountains, having told no one where I was? I thought about my mother the whole night and was confronted with my selfishness. In the middle of the night, I opened my medical kit and started taking antibiotics. With whiskey. That really helped.

The following day I dragged my body up several valleys, crisscrossed many rivers and eventually slogged my way over the snow-covered ridge. The staggering views of the M'Goun massif with the summit of *Ighil M'Goun* (4,068m) towering high above, remains imprinted in my memory!

It was late afternoon when I finally started descending the *Rougoult* pass to the village of *Amezri*. I made my way to a small Berber inn where I was again met with so much compassion. Despite being unable to speak an intelligible word with my hosts, I received gestures of help: warm food, a shower and a place to roll out my sleeping bag. I dozed off that night, *so* alone, but so sure of the love of God.

The next day on my way out of the valley, I was invited to a Moroccan Berber house. Mint tea, lots of gesticulation, laughing and kids wanting to take pics with me. A strange and enriching experience of common humanity.

This solo hike over the M'Goun Mountains helped me to articulate some serious and underlying issues that surfaced during my year in London.

I was *really* lonely that year - albeit surrounded by some of the best people in my life. Certain experiences we go through, we endure completely alone, even within a community. I believe we find beauty and strength when we are able to hear each other using the same words and speaking the same language. Indeed, kindness and expressions of solicitude help more than one can articulate. But it does not mend loneliness when what you're going through is something that no-one around you can relate to.

This transitional space is often referred to as *liminality* - an experience of occupying a position at, or on both sides of a threshold. Neither of which you really belong to.

Anymore.

5

SPACE BETWEEN

*"We're strange allies
With warring hearts
What a wild-eyed beast you be
The space between…"*

- Dave Matthews

In May 2008 I started reading what felt like *everything* I could find about Ancient Hebrew.

Most of it was internet resources, but I also managed to procure some printed material. Since I didn't have much guidance on this new-found path, I devoured any and everything as potential building blocks to construct a working model of this "new" language.

First, there was a new alphabet. And very soon I discovered that this so-called 'Hebrew Alphabet' had several historical varieties - all of which featured for short but specific bursts on the Middle Eastern timeline.

I discovered that all of these variants, ranging from ancient *pictographs* to the complete new syncretised version after the Jewish exile to Babylon (586 BCE to 522 BCE), were drawn or written from right to left.

It was a lot to take in. And then there was the all-pervasive reality that these Hebrew building blocks - whether pictures or letters - all had intrinsic meaning related to the culture and worldview of the ancient desert dwellers.

I found myself not only trying to memorise and come to terms with novel letters and pictures but also with completely new concepts about life!

It was quite striking how the pictographs of the older Hebrew alphabet conveyed meaning to basic words: the almost over-simplified way that combined pictures gave expression to life as the Ancients lived it. Then I could discover how the Ancient Hebrew language was constructed, from simple root concepts to complex idiomatic expressions.

I realised that my understanding of Ancient Hebrew would require me to step *out* of my known reality, and *into* a world that was fundamentally different in nearly every single aspect.

I was fascinated. And swept along by a current that I was not going to get out of…

Language and culture are inextricably linked. *Language is defined as "a system or method of communication…consisting of the use of words* in a structured and conventional way… as used by a *particular community."* For this very reason, a study of any language means a study of its host culture. Now to reiterate an interesting point, Ancient Hebrew had never been a stand-alone language; at least not for long continuous periods of time.

When we consider the history of the Hebrew language, we soon discover that Abraham - the first to be called a *Hebrew* ("HA'IVRIT". See Genesis 14:13 for context) - was someone from a far-away region, towards the east of Canaan.

Abraham was originally a native of the city of *Ur* of the Chaldeans - some 225 km southeast of the site of Babylon in southern Mesopotamia. He is outlined as a stranger called by Yahweh out of *Haran* (see Genesis 11:31) to the land of

Canaan. The Biblical account relays his obedience and sojourning. He eventually makes his way west and southwards to the land of Canaan. In Hebrew, this word "KENA'AN" means 'humiliated' or 'lowland'. The literal meaning refers to the 'land below' the level of the sea.

Abraham was the first to receive the promise and covenant that Yahweh would bless and establish his offspring. Although he was deemed the progenitor of the Hebrews, Abraham himself did *not* speak Hebrew. His native language was a Sumerian dialect, probably altered by his travels and sojourning in Haran and Egypt, and eventually his intermingling with the Canaanite people.

This amalgamation of various cultural and language facets eventually found a home in the land later known as *Israel*, and this was how Ancient Hebrew was born: a syncretism between Babylonian (Assyrian), Canaanite, Phoenician and Egyptian building blocks… amongst many others.

The common cultural denominator of the people who contributed to this new language was a lifestyle exemplified by everything *nomadic*. This refers to a desert-dwelling people who valued family and livestock as their most prized possessions. They lived as shepherds rather than cultivators, and their common enemy and the biggest drive was to find water and graze land under harsh conditions. For nomads, shelter did not mean buildings, but tents.

Following prescribed journeys in pursuit of food and water shaped people who understood navigation based on the stars and distinct desert landmarks. This temporal approach to almost everything shaped their cultural intimations. The language we casually refer to as Ancient Hebrew is *permeated* with the reality of a nomadic people and their worldview. And curiously, this is the language that our Creator chose for the entire Hebrew Biblical narrative.

It took me very long to come to terms with this uncomfortable truth. And looking back, I slowly began to understand why God uprooted my own life in such a similar fashion. As my journey continues to unfold, I realise that experiencing something of a nomadic worldview is pivotal to sharing this language with others.

With the exception of two or three years, I have basically been living as a nomad since 2008.

ISRAEL

I arrived at Ben Gurion Airport in Tel Aviv on the 10th of April 2009. Apart from my childlike excitement to finally be *there*, I remember the strangest feeling of *déjà vu*.
I've been here before…

The *Egged* service to East Talpiot was doing its scheduled sunset route. I got off at a bus stop in what seemed like a peaceful but affluent neighbourhood and eagerly walked down the road. The keys to the Raz family's front door were exactly where they said it would be, hidden barely out of sight.

The evening was cooler than expected. I was grateful that a family I know only through meeting their daughter at an airport in South America would allow me to stay alone in their house for ten days!

I slowly opened the large wooden door where a life-sized Buddha statue awaited me. In that moment it struck me that reality was far from straightforward. Israel may have *many* more layers than I naively assumed.

The only person I knew in the land, was my friend *Arava* whom I met at Punta Arenas airport the year before.

It was a Friday afternoon. At the time I had been celebrating the weekly Shabbat for almost a year, but I had no inkling that an entire country shuts down with the onset of a Friday evening.

I phoned Arava who's number I luckily had saved. Weirdly enough, she picked up *and* she remembered me. She had a good laugh at my lack of cultural preparation.

Arava was across the border in Jordan at the time, and her folks were travelling in South America. She prompted me to give her some time to phone her parents. And minutes later she returned my call and offered their house to me! Within my first hour in Israel, a random Jewish family opened their entire house to a complete stranger. I was only going to comprehend this level of kindness to strangers' years down the line.

NEIGHBOURS

A little background to my first trip to Israel: my good friend and mentor, Michael Hack, invited me to an *Operation Mobilisation* retreat in Beirut, Lebanon, when he learned that I'd be in the Middle East during that time.

We made our plans and I decided that after exploring Jerusalem for a week or so, I'd attempt an overland trip from Israel to Jordan, and then from Jordan to Syria with the hope of reaching the *OM* team in Beirut within a couple of days. Little did either of us know that roaming between Israel, Syria and Lebanon was impossible. The *only* serious matter that Mike raised at the time was, "Do not tell anyone that you are coming from Israel."

Upon her return to Israel my friend Arava spent some days showing me around the Old City of Jerusalem. I felt a surreal cognisance of '*finally* I was in the Land!'

A myriad of smells, sounds, and architecture hit the senses. The atmosphere was loaded with tension, and perplexing history… Jerusalem cannot be described; she simply has to be experienced.

I felt at home. For almost a week Arava took me to explore all the hidden nooks and hinterlands of Jerusalem. It was magical. Little did I know then that this icon of a city, would one day become a 'second home'…

My adventure to Beirut began with a bus ride from Jerusalem to the city of Beit She'an in the northeast of Israel. Beit She'an is best known in the Bible for the place where King Saul and three of his sons' bodies were hung on the city walls, following the war between Israel and the Philistines on Mount Gilboa (See 1 Sam 31:10-12).

The bus dropped me off in Beit She'an with soaring temperatures in the 30's Celsius coupled with extreme humidity. The *Sheikh Hussein* Bridge is the northern-most of three border crossings between Israel and Jordan and is situated about 10km outside Beit She'an. I arrived at the border with a backpack full of camping and recording equipment, hair shaven to my scalp and… solo. Which is still how I roll. I crossed the border without any problems.

On the other side I withdrew some Jordanian Dirham from an ATM and quickly found a taxi to drive me straight to the Jordan-Syria border post. What struck me was how incredibly expensive Jordan was compared to Israel. I only had a limited budget, and my taxi ride from the Sheikh Hussein Bridge swallowed a sizeable chunk of my cash.

In those days, as a result of the political tension between Israel and her neighbours, Israeli immigration stamps were offered on loose papers that one could remove from your passport, erasing any trace of the Holy Land from your travels. But one had to specifically ask for it. This often resulted in a serious interrogation from immigration officials. I had both my Jordanian Visa and my little Israeli immigration stamp on loose pieces of paper.

The taxi drove me into the sunset, with the beautiful Jordanian landscape captivating my senses as the hazy afternoon turned to dusk. It was *much* further to the Syrian border than I expected, and by the time we reached the almost inconspicuous crossing, it was pitch dark.

My taxi driver, who was not fluent in English, dropped me at the Jordanian side, and proceeded to do his paperwork. We were one of a few other vehicles at the border. A friendly Jordanian official asked me where I was heading. "Damascus, and then onwards to Beirut in Lebanon," I gregariously responded. "You know that you are not allowed into Syria with an Israeli stamp?" I nodded in agreement, pretending I had considered all the limitations. I hadn't…

About a hundred meters from the Jordanian immigration office stood the small building of the Syrian counterpart. My taxi driver parked outside and sent me to collect my Syrian stamp.

Except for the large Syrian official, I was the only other person at the counter. "Passport." I handed the man my Dutch passport, which he scrutinised from front to back several times. "Where is your Jordanian Visa?"

I confidently pointed out, "It's in there!" To which the official responded impatiently, "There is nothing in here." At that moment, many things went through my mind. Earlier, the guy on the Jordanian side of the crossing tried to warn me of the dilemma of travelling between Israel and any of her neighbours. Perhaps he took both my Israeli immigration stamp as well as my Jordanian Visa.

I took back my passport and started paging for the Jordanian Visa… Gone. And then his question dropped, "Where did you come from?"

This was happening at almost 22:00, and I was alone on the Syrian side of an unwelcome border crossing, with *no* mobile phone reception. My taxi driver came in at that point, telling me I needed to hurry up…

The Syrian official's mood changed for the worse, "Did you come from Israel?"

Michael's words resonated in my ears. But I was not going to lie. I said nothing and just stared back at the guy. He took my passport, "Wait here." And left.

I waited for 20 minutes. My taxi driver came in and told me he was leaving me. Which he did.

The Syrian official returned with a big black book and started writing in Arabic shorthand, every bit of detail from my passport. I felt scrutinized and also gripped by fear. This might be my end. I desperately wanted to phone my parents, or anyone - but I couldn't.

The Syrian man's silence was ominous as he made several annotations in his big book. Then he said, "Follow me." I took my pack and followed him down a dimmed hallway…

Heart pounding. We came to a backdoor where a car was waiting for me. "Get in..." I reluctantly got in the back of what felt like a Syrian taxi and we took off. About two minutes later the car stopped and the driver told me to get out. He drove off as I tried to orientate myself in the dark.

In the distance, I could distinguish the Jordanian border post building. I started walking towards it. It was nearly 23:00. A janitor inside the dimly lit building was sweeping the floor. I knocked on the window and he made his way to me without hesitation.

"Excuse me sir, can you *please* help me..." My own voice sounded timorous as I tried to explain to him that I had lost two official papers here earlier. And there they were: my blue Israeli Immigration paper and Jordanian Visa were lying right there in a small filing box.

I arrived back in Jordan at a hotel in *Amman* somewhere past midnight. I spent the remainder of the evanescent night in a run-down little room, reeking of urine, still unable to let any of my loved ones know where I was. I was also anxious to get in contact with the O.M. crew in Beirut. Early the next morning I got on a bus from Amman back to the Sheikh Hussein border post. I sat next to a Muslim man who started talking to me about God. At the time I was unsure of how to pitch my religion. Our discussion went on for hours until we reached the border.

I was interrogated on the Jordanian side of the border crossing for about 90 minutes before they let me through. But it really was on the Israeli side that I learned just what border security meant.

The border police made me sit on the floor and asked me the same odd questions about my family every 30 minutes, for seven hours. The soldiers rotated but the questions remained the same. They did not like the idea that I carried microphones and a laptop. I eventually convinced them that I was a music producer by composing a piece of music right there on the floor using only my Mac.

It was dark by the time I received my re-entry stamp for Israel. It was also a Friday evening again. And not only was it the weekly Shabbat, it also happened to be the Feast of Passover! You really *do not* want to be stuck 40 kilometres from the town you're heading to, at 21:00 on a Friday night of the Feast of Unleavened Bread...

An Arab taxi driver proposed to take me to Tiberias (the largest city on the Western shore of the Sea of Galilee) for a $100. Since that was all the money I had left after my Jordan-Syria ordeal, I refused his offer and started walking in the direction of Beit She'an at around 22:00. An Israeli official warned me that walking along the Israel-Jordan border might not be the wisest idea but since I had no other options, I took off into the humid night...

About an hour later I heard the strangest noise behind me. I spun around, and out of the dark, a tall figure made his appearance... Let's call him *Scott* (since I really cannot remember his name) ... Scott was a 21-year-old American security officer who served in Baghdad for a season. Scott introduced himself and told me that the taxi driver also wanted to charge him $100, which he also couldn't afford. So, Scott and I decided that we were going to try and reach Tiberias by sunrise; after all we only had 35-odd kilometres left to go!

In the hours that followed we exchanged travel stories that made the time fly by. I recall how Scott told me about his near-jail experiences which rendered my mountaineering trips pale in comparison.

Around midnight the same Arab taxi stopped next to us… realising that these young men were going to walk all the way, he offered us a ride to Tiberias for $10 each.

We took it.

Upon our arrival in Tiberias, we were surrounded with a Passover *simcha*, celebrations that felt nothing short of hedonistic: loud Israeli music, dancing, cannabis… I was exhausted after 48 hours of non-stop travel. Scott wanted to know where I was intending to stay for the night. Both of us had no budget. I told him that I was going to try and find a spot on the Galilee lakeshore to sleep. He asked me to mark the place where I would be camping with a yellow ribbon. I eventually found a spot and tied a yellow cord to a tree. Sneaking through an open gate I rolled my sleeping bag onto a putt-putt turf behind a hotel. The night's rest was sweet. I never saw Scott again.

Early the next morning the gardener rudely woke me up. I had slept almost right on the water's edge and rose to the ineffable first light breaking over the Sea of Galilee - the lake that Yeshua walked on, the shores which host so many timeless Biblical stories.

I stayed on for a few days at the Aviv Hostel close to the lakeshore in Tiberias. Here I remember meeting two young lady travellers from Germany. We spoke about the love and character of Jesus… And as we were exchanging viewpoints, I was struck by how delving into Judaism that year had left my heart callous. It stood in sharp contrast to their simple faith and contagious love.

Some days later I bumped into the same two ladies on the top of Masada! As if the Father *really* wanted to drive the point home…

Back in Jerusalem I met up with Mike and the O.M. team that arrived from Beirut. It was incredible to catch up with Mike - who had played an enormous role in my spiritual foundation over the years - and share our first impressions of the Land of Israel.

From Jerusalem to Masada to the Dead Sea and some time in Haifa… three weeks flew by. I left with a very different impression of Israel than I had anticipated.

My takeaway from that first encounter was that a mere academic view on the Land and the God of Israel was not going to help me in the long run. My heart had grown stone cold, and I needed a reintroduction to the true, Biblical figure known as *Yeshua* the Messiah.

I returned to England for a few days, to pack up my nomadic life in New Malden, and fly home.

Whatever *home* meant.

LIMINALITY

In the process of unpacking the truth about my journey, I discovered that *loneliness* was, and remains, an almost negligible facet of a more abstruse matter.

I was introduced to the term *liminality* through a book called "Exiles: Living Missionally in a Post-Christian Culture" (2006) by Australian author Michael Frost.

Liminality, in short, is a *transitional* experience.

In his publication *"Rites de Passage"* (1909), Arnold van Gennep - the father of the concept of liminality - suggests that every rite of passage follows a three-fold structure, regardless of culture.

The first is called the 'stage of separation' (*"preliminal rite"*), followed by a 'middle stage' known as the *"liminal rite"*, and concludes with a 'stage of reincorporation' or *"postliminal rite"*.

As I dove into the deeper strata of the *loneliness* theme, I discovered that big chunks of my own journey's passage were synonymous with being stuck in a 'liminal rite'. Not because of any external factor *per se*, but more so because of my own inability to consummate various transitional rites…

The idea of living transitionally has always appealed to me. But for the greater part of my life, I had mistaken the *ephemeral* for what was, indeed, a perpetual way of life. What was meant to be interim experiences of vicissitude, I have come to think of as home. My heart has suffered greatly because of this incessant lack of true belonging.

HOME

My wonder-woman mother, Rina, is a native Capetonian. She turned 79 recently although she acts and looks as if she is in her 50's!

My incredibly musical, Dutch father, Pieter Meijer († 1938 - 2015), immigrated to South Africa in 1966. He met my mother some years later, and they got married on the 29th of March 1974, after dating for only a few months.

Mother was, and still is, a devout believer. As their story goes, she discovered on their honeymoon that my dad did not believe in God. Nowadays this phenomenon isn't surprising at all, but it *was* in 1974. Even more so because he was a dedicated church organist.

My amazing sister Carla was born on February the 17th, 1975. She and I grew up in a ménage where God was *not* central. My parents were both church musicians but at different congregations. As a result, my sister and I attended different Sunday services, either with mom or dad. At times Carla and I would split up, each joining one of our parents. As a kid, I remember that this felt normal, but not right. But *what* was right?

It would take me almost all of my adult life to realise that parents need to have a unified voice when it comes to substantial matters.

I gave my life to Yeshua when I was 12 years old. I was alone in our kitchen one summer's night, and I suddenly became aware of the overwhelming love of God. The details have grown asunder over the years, but I still remember the simple surrender and incredible joy. I never made anything of the fact that there wasn't any hype around it. That lone wolf moment, for good or bad, became a pattern for much of my faith journey.

I was inextricably drawn to God as a young boy. Throughout the ebbs and flows of growing up, this yearning has never gone away.

My dad and I had a curious connection. I always wanted to win him over. I think he enjoyed my independent style, even in pursuing God, as if in *that* aspect of our interaction, his reciprocal respect reposed.

Mother's faith was naive and contagious although her worldview is very different from mine. I always gravitated slightly more towards my dad's introverted personality, which was strongly reflected in his approach to music.

Our family's idiosyncratic faith impacted my life dramatically. On the downside, it translated into a journey where I didn't fit in either with the religious, or naughty kids. I had a sincere yearning to find and follow God but did not fit the example I saw in the church kids. I felt lonely and without a sense of belonging.

'Lone wolf' was, and remains, the obvious critique although much good was born from this.

I was the boy who walked around with a pocket Bible in my blazer, spending every bit of time I had on my own simply reading. My faith in God became robust albeit driven by a strong belief I still don't even comprehend.

Towards the second half of my High School years, I was strolling between two classes, lost in thought when my Afrikaans teacher walked up to me and declared that I would be preaching to school kids in the near future. I did not understand this decree, but at the end of that year, I was elected chairman of our school's Christian Student Association and the following year I found myself leading up to five prayer meetings a week.

Because of my new-found responsibility, I spent countless nights reading the Bible, uncovering layers and themes which shaped *in* me a Bible teacher of sorts.

At least a handful of schoolteachers were in support of the young speaker in the making. So much so, that later that same year I was elected head boy of the school. The confidence borne from the many speaking engagements that year probably was the tipping point for my selection.

Joining a missionary outreach into Africa during my final year at school, I felt that my road ahead was to become a full-time missionary. Even my parents entertained the idea for a while, but whichever way I evaluate my unconventional journey of faith, the road was *lonely*.

When I returned to South Africa in 2009, I moved back into my old house in Brandwacht Street in Stellenbosch and although many things were back to normal (making music, running in the mountains, doing life with friends), I did arrive back from London with a new-found perspective on life. I quit working on the Sabbath, simply because I had *tasted* something of the freedom that came with it. Very soon after being back in Stellenbosch, I was asked by my former congregation to join the team of elders. I was the youngest of twelve, but it was an enormous privilege which I embraced gladly.

We met often, and I discovered in those first couple of months just how complicated it is to run a church! During that same time but quite on the opposite side of my faith-life, I invited friends to Shabbat-meals on Friday evenings. Some of my closest friends were open to and embraced the newness of it all. But I lost many through the unconventional prodding of what felt to them like Jewish tradition: under the law.

This spiritual tension during the first years back in South Africa was truly uncomfortable. I was constantly trying to reconcile two worlds that were essentially disconnected. Even divided.

On the one end I tried to introduce and integrate some of the beautiful Hebraic principles into the eldership team I was now part of, and on the other hand, I passionately undertook to introduce friends and family to Shabbat. In many ways it felt like I failed on both accounts, all the while finding myself more detached from everything that seemed to be my previous 'normal'.

Ironically, an essential part of me *loved* the conundrum.

About two years after joining the church eldership, the tension between my beliefs and reality became unbearable, and I resigned. Part of my conviction at the time was to undertake a short detox from the institutional church. This decision eventually rendered me unable to return and effectively accentuated everything liminal.

LIMINAL MUSIC

My journey to Morocco in March 2009, translated into me writing and producing a solo *cello* album for my friend Carol Thorns, which in turn veered me into composing and producing a solo *harp* album for Shelley Frost in Dubai, and a solo album for Capetonian saxophonist Judy Brown. In a number of ways, these three projects embodied my passion for fusing classical, electronic and Middle Eastern music.

During this time, I was approached to compose theme music for one of the largest fashion retail conglomerates in South Africa, as well as for a massive mining company on the West Coast. This was above and beyond a rather fully booked production schedule. I really felt that my life as a music producer and composer was coming to perfect fulfilment.

In July 2011 I visited the Netherlands with my dad. He was already quite ill with cancer. But of the scores of amazing happenings in my short earthly life, those three weeks in the Netherlands with my dad stand out tall, especially in the light of our disarticulated journeys. We were offered a chance to connect with each other and with our greater Dutch family in a way that otherwise would never have materialised, thanks to Yahweh's provision through the music. I knew at the time that in the future I would think back on this with fondness. Now is the future.

In 2012 I moved in with my friend Nicole (this is not her first name). I needed a lock-up-and-go of sorts and she owned the perfect little congenial hub in town, which went by the tag 'Fabulous Formosa'. I had a bedroom and a small recording studio in her house, and weirdly enough our completely contrasting personality-styles afforded us effortless and harmonious coexistence. To say the least, we became really good friends. Maybe partly because we both have Dutch backgrounds. We shared a community, great humour and a list of similarities in terms of lifestyle. I appreciate Nicole's peerless devotion to our friendship - something I regrettably could not see for its potential at the time due to my blindfolded *idée fixe* of other humans.

I embarked on a project called "In Verwondering" with fellow musicians Louis Brittz, Retief Burger and my friend Neil Büchner. We rigged a small project studio in a farmhouse in Sutherland and spent three days and nights writing songs inspired by the night skies and the handiwork of God! *In Verwondering* left quite a mark in Christian music circles, but for me, the bliss of the project boiled down to writing songs about God, with good friends under Karoo skies.

Towards the latter part of the year, I received a random phone call from an old friend, Emile. We met in 2007, he got married, I moved to London and we lost contact. Emile informed me about his crumbling marriage and within days, he moved into the flat behind Nicole's house. Emile and I picked up the pieces on a number of faith-related matters and we soon realised that all of what was unfolding was a godsend.

In 2013 we managed to get our hands on the old Brandwacht house again, and it soon became a sort of family home for our growing but liminal faith community. That year we celebrated Shabbat almost every Friday with weird and wonderful people. We observed the Biblical feasts, we studied the Word, we held dinners, we ran in the mountains, we slept on the floors without beds... and had one insanely joyous year!

But not everyone appreciated our strange faith community. I began picking up on cultish references amongst my friends, and it really did not help matters when a small bunch of us made known that we were planning to move to Israel the following year for an investigation of the Hebrew *Shmitah*.

We didn't fit in with society that year and our radical convictions were about to become even more bizarre.

Towards the end of 2013, I met a beautiful, free-spirited girl that I will call Lillian. Lillian and I never dated, but over the course of more than three years, we became extremely close, although sadly our shared journey (at least from my perspective) followed several of the same unhealthy patterns as my former entanglement with Michaela. Barefoot artist with dreadlocks - Lillian was a textbook gipsy: unbound, energetic and filled with a contagious love for people.

She personified much of the freedom I've always longed for but never found the courage to pursue. I fell in love with Lillian on such a deep level and my heart took several years of additional pounding, but today I consider our shared journey worth more than the heartache it caused. Maybe because her ingress into my life marked a visceral end to what felt like a never-ending emotional tussle with Michaela.

Lillian ended up joining our small band of nomads to Israel in 2014. Our journeys continued somewhat parallel during that year and also thereafter, but over time we gradually drifted into separate destinies.

As much as I was left perplexed with all the *why's*, I deem myself incredibly privileged by the more than three exceptional years we roamed together. Suffice to say, I was granted massive extrication through Lillian's total lightness of being in my life.

At times I still mourn our separation.

7

SEVEN

*"I was blind but now I see
What if God is not for me
And I know, it's time to go*

*I've been used
And I've been played
I've been spied on and betrayed
And I know, it's time to go..."*

- Enigma

Most people I know never stop.

Our culture extols *busyness* (I wonder whether 'busyness' and 'business' are related concepts), and society at large holds us in esteem when the days of our lives are marked by *striving!* The harder we strive, the more we are lauded for being goal-driven, self-motivated, living with purpose…

When this ardent lifestyle of chasing every next item on the itinerary is coupled with always being online, incessant social media engagement, fast-food, addictions, compromised sleeping, broken relationships, financial insecurity, anxiety… and *voilà*! Not only are we constantly overwhelmed, we live low-quality lives marked by mere survival. And in most cases, we simply die young.

For obscure reasons, the theme of 'rest' is not celebrated in society at large. "We'll sleep when we're dead!" we say. Very few of us are immune to the malady of striving. Not even followers of Christ. Maybe it's because we don't like being told what to do… "We're not under the Law!" Yet our lives hardly demonstrate any form of real freedom. Our self-preservation is on *our own* terms.

"The ego hates losing. Even unto to God." - Richard Rohr.

I discovered something of the Biblical counter-culture invitation proposed to us through the weekly Shabbat, and even through the *seven* festivals of Yahweh. But nothing lured me into the reassuring goodness of God like the *Shmitah* or Hebrew Sabbatical Year.

Outlined in detail in Exodus 23, Leviticus 25 and Deuteronomy 15, the purpose of the *Shmitah* is two-fold.

Firstly, it is a year of letting the ground rest:

> *"...for six years you are to sow your land,*
> *and shall gather its increase,*
> *but the seventh year you are to let it rest,*
> *and shall leave it,*
> *and the poor of your people shall eat.*
> *And what they leave, the beasts of the field eat.*
> *Do the same with your vineyard and your olive grove."*
> *- Exodus 23:10-11*

And secondly, it is a year concluded by a release:

> *"At the end of seven years you will enact a release..."*
> *- Deuteronomy 15:1*

This word "SHMITAH" - derived from the verb "SHAMAT" which means "to release" or "let drop" - refers to the "release" or "remission" of debt in concrete terms. Although the effect of the *Shmitah* only comes at the end of a seven-year period, the year is known as the "Year of Release" (Heb. *Sh'nat Shmitah*) and therefore refers to every seventh year in its entirety:

'A year of rest,...and letting go of debt.'

This is quite a bohemian concept for a perpetually burnt-out society that profits from its people being in debt!

SEVEN

Numbers in Hebrew are very important. A handful of numerical values occur more abundantly than others in the Biblical text, and these often escape our attention because they don't necessarily mean anything in our guest cultures.

The numbers 1, 3, 6, 7, 12, 40 and 50 all seem to occur quite frequently, but it's the number 7 that stands out.

The Hebrew noun for 'seven' is "SHEVA" and this curious Hebrew word not only points to the cardinal number but also literally means "oath" or "promise".

Genesis 21 relays the story of Abraham (whose seventh generation descendent was Moses) entering into a covenant with the Philistine king, *Avimelech*. Abraham's shepherds dug a well and after a dispute of ownership, Abraham presented Avimelech with seven lambs as testimony that he dug the well. The two entered into a covenant and the well was named "BE'ER SHEVA":

"Well of Seven" or "Well of [an] Oath".

The verbal form of *sheva* reveals the hidden link, as it literally means "to swear" or "to be complete".

With this important linguistic pointer in mind, when we now look at how very specific Biblical events are tied to the number 'seven', things start to make sense.

The seventh and last day of every week is set apart (given a different but specific function or purpose) as the Sabbath. In Hebrew, the days of the week are simply named after their respective nominal numbers (e.g. first day, third day, sixth day etc.), except for the seventh day, called the "SHABBAT". The Shabbat not only concludes the week, but it also makes it 'complete' as in the sense of a full-stop at the end of a sentence.

The seventh month is host to three of the most prominent Hebrew festivals: *Yom Teru'ah* ("Day of Sounding"), *Yom HaKippurim* or simply *Yom Kippur* ("Day of [the] Covering") and the well-known festival of *Sukkot* ("Booths" or "Tabernacles"). Quite simply, of the seven Hebrew festivals, the seventh month completes the annual cycle of festivals with the Feast of *Sukkot* - celebrating that the Messiah will one day dwell eternally with His people - completing the cycle of so-called 'dress rehearsals' or 'appointed times'.

Likewise, the seventh year - known as the *Shmitah* - concludes a seven-year cycle. And seven of these seven-year cycles (or 49 years) inaugurate the Year of Jubilee (Heb. *Yovel*), or the fiftieth year. The Jubilee cycle is the greatest of the epochs found in the text.

Apart from the obvious repetitions found in the Hebraic worldview, the idea that certain days, months and years mark the end or fulfilment of events and times, is the point of the number 'seven'.

There is a whole lot more to this matter. And we're not even touching on the number 'seven' as it occurs in the Apostolic Writings (aka the "New Testament") but suffice to say that whenever we are faced with *sheva* in the Hebrew Bible, we should pay special attention.

This was the insight that Emile and I were confronted with in 2013 when we both felt convinced that we should not turn a blind eye to the upcoming *Shmitah*. We believed that if we were to have a valid opinion of the *Shmitah*, would need to *experience* it… *in* the land of Israel.

I remember the day that we compared notes - or shall I say 'convictions'. We had more or less one year to get our ducks in a row before the *Shmitah* would commence in March 2014.

We ploughed an immense amount of emotional and physical verve into the decision to quit jobs, sell cars, pack up our lives and move to Israel for an entire year. During that same time, we also discovered that the upcoming *Shmitah* was year 49 (the seventh of seven cycles of seven years) of a 50-year Jubilee cycle. This meant that two consecutive sabbatical years were lining up! (This, happens only once in most people's lives.)

As our departure in 2014 drew near, we managed to expand our little *Shmitah*-group to ten people. Emile and I shared the responsibility of procuring air tickets for most of the team. The two of us were yoked together as the conveners of the team, even if only from a vanguard point of view.

During those months of preparation, Emile and Jana (one of three doctors on our team) got engaged! This layer added to the intricacy of our maiden voyage ahead. No pun intended!

A lot happened during those last couple of months before our departure. We left for Israel in a whirlwind. At the time we were too consumed by the practicalities of our trip to realise what we were actually getting into.

I visited my parents before we left South Africa. The day that we greeted was the most broken-hearted I ever saw my dad. He was very ill of cancer. We both knew that our farewell might very well be our last goodbyes. I sobbed all the way back to Stellenbosch.

I am sure that day left a deep hurt in both of us.

DEVORAH

21 March 2014.

Getting all of us and our luggage on the Turkish Airways flight to Tel Aviv was nothing short of comical. How much nonsense does one need for a year, knowing full-well that our monetary resources might run out?

We arrived at Ben Gurion Airport in the middle of the night, more than 24 hours after our departure. My good friend Pierre and I were the designated drivers of our rental cars to a small village called *Devorah* in the centre of the country. I have known Pierre since we were four years old. It was the longest two-hour drive ever. I fell asleep behind the wheel more than once. But we made it.

"DEVORAH" is a "bee" in Hebrew. And *Devorah* is also the cutest little *moshav* (like a kibbutz, but where families and individuals work towards their own profit) in the Jezre'el Valley, some 60 km west of the Sea of Galilee.

We arrived at daybreak. Two fully loaded cars. The months of preparation, appeasing family and friends, storing and selling stuff… were finally over. Our friendly host took us to our rooms, and we slept for almost the entire day.

We arrived in Israel a few days prior to the start of the Biblical New Year: the 1st of Aviv, 2014. Our decision to reach the Land early enough made sense considering the bigger picture of being 'there' when the calendar ticks over.

But *Devorah* was to become a strange and once-again liminal experience. At least for Emile and me.

Our stay in the village was quite comfortable. We had shared rooms, a place to cook, and there was a swimming pool and also big open fields for running. All we needed!

Those first couple of days revolved around one shared evening meal. We soon realised that having a joint objective in Israel did not make it easier to cook a meal for ten strangers. Matters were also complicated because we were not transparent about our financial affairs as a group. That, at least, was my assessment of the situation.

We were going through intense personal transitions. Emile and I hardly spoke during that first week in *Devorah*. I was very much perturbed. We were such amazing friends but financially we were inconveniently yoked together.

Six days into our stay, Emile had a chat with me about feeling uncomfortable regarding our finances. He was convinced that God told him to sever his financial ties with me. At that time the two of us were almost completely intertwined in the *Shmitah* affair. For some months prior to our departure we shared resources quite nimbly. This contributed significantly to my credit card debt. For this reason, his one-sided verdict caught me utterly off-guard. Moreover, our group took it for granted that Emile and I were in unity, at *least* in the area of our monetary resources.

This is but my one-sided take on the matter… And again, the only fair truth would be to hear both of our chronicles.

After a week we left for Jerusalem and it was there that the proverbial bomb exploded. Emile and I had a confrontation and I realised then that for me to survive, I would need to pack up and return home. It was mortifying to discuss this with the team in a transparent manner especially since I was one of the orchestrators. But in one accord, the group persuaded me to stay.

Emile was obviously and understandably entwined with his wife-to-be, while I was yoked together with some of the team members who decided to stick with me. Effectively, our group bifurcated within the first two weeks in Israel.

Almost two months of this lamentable reality passed.

During this time, we had some sort of normality. We explored the land far and wide, from multi-day hikes, camping on lakeshores and hostel-roofs, exploring mountains, deserts and seas, to making the most amazing new friends. Tal and Einam Avishai deserve to be singled out for their boundless love and hospitality towards the entire bunch of us.

Unfortunately, after two and a half months in Israel, a handful of us returned to South Africa for our infamous border-jump. Not many of us returned.

I arrived back from Israel with a shattered friendship, but also with accumulated credit card debt of almost R140k. My dad was severely ill, and to make matters worse, a few of my friends confronted me saying they could not make peace with the fact that I was openly 'throwing away my life'.

They also insisted on a defence of my views surrounding the Israel-Palestinian saga. Put bluntly, I was framed as a geopolitical advocate for Israel. And something of the depth of misunderstanding surrounding our decision to investigate the *Shmitah*, only dawned on me then. But from this awkward confrontation, I decided to take up the challenge of familiarizing myself with the Palestinian view of Israel.

I went to visit my parents in our hometown for about two weeks. During this time, I spent many hours seeking out trustworthy sources with the objective to balance my viewpoint.

It was during one of these searches that I stumbled upon a gripping YouTube account of a Christian Palestinian's stance on the tension between Palestine and Israel. I watched her clip and was spellbound. My dad agreed to watch it with me for a second time. And I remember he was equally fascinated. One of the strangest moments in my life, which eventually turned into a reality, was that after watching Christy Anastas' YouTube talk twice, I had the conviction that we were going to meet and be *in* each other's lives for the rest of our days.

Christy's story of political asylum was adrenaline for my restless pursuit of the truth and exactly what I'd been looking for. I struggled to sleep that night.

Early the next day I began my search for her. And within the hour, I reached a gentleman in the UK who nonchalantly provided me with Christy's email address. Let's call him Harold.

I emailed her immediately, she responded, and she allotted me a 45-minute Skype slot almost 7 weeks down the line. I made sure to pencil it in.

I arrived back in Israel with two members of our original group at the end of July for another 3-month stint. In many ways, our second departure was stranger than the first. The team was now fragmented, and I also didn't know whether I'd see my dad alive again.

But... I returned to Israel debt-free. Barely four months into our journey, the promise of *Shmitah* was already being fulfilled.

Emile and Jana rented a small apartment in downtown Jerusalem, and in the spirit of reconciliation, the three of us were invited to stay with them for a couple of nights. It was healing on some level. But the delusion that had crept into my friendship with Emile was still lurking beneath the surface.

We planned a cycle tour of the land that would take us around seven weeks. We bought bicycles and some bare necessities and spent most of our time together attempting to overcome the elephant in the room.

We left together as a united group but sadly the bomb exploded again between 'us and them', which convinced me that whatever was not okay between us was not going to be solved easily. We mournfully parted ways in a total lack of peace.

Danielle, Madeleine and I started cycling at the Zemach junction - the southernmost point of the Sea of Galilee. The midsummer's heat was sweltering, but we managed to cycle to Kibbutz *Ein Gev* - a slightly more modern expression of what you get used to in terms of *Kibbutzim* (Hebrew plural for a kibbutz) in Israel.

We camped right on the stony beach of the Sea of Galilee. My excitement to be on our long-awaited adventure was coupled with the anticipation of my Skype call with Christy Anastas in London the next morning.

Over the course of the weeks that followed, the three of us ate out of the hand of God. Not a single day on our trip was there *not* enough money in our bank accounts to buy food. Against all odds, our cash never ran out. Moreover, we were invited for random coffees by roadsides, into campsites, into people's backyards and into their homes... During the almost two months we cycled, we experienced the gift of *Shmitah* in such a visceral way.

CHRISTY ANASTAS

"Christy! My name is Helmut. I am a South African on a sabbatical in Israel hoping to make some kind of documentary about the *Shmitah* year, and I would love to hear your story."

This is how our six-year friendship began. I sat down at the restaurant at Ein Gev, and 45 minutes of intuitive dialogue left me in a daze. During the last few minutes of our conversation, I asked Christy how I could help her: I had time to think, pray and even do stuff. She responded that not many people ever offer her help; it's mostly the other way around. She still says that *that* was the turn-around for her.

I was struck by our fascinating conversation, but also intrigued by this human. Christy allowed me to have her Skype number only… Understandably so.

Christy was a law student in Bethlehem at the time of the Second Intifada (also called the "Al-Aqsa Intifada"). She began probing the Scriptures for insight regarding the various people groups' claims on the Land. As a young female Palestinian student, her curiosity and her subsequent change in attitude towards Israelis were not appreciated by her community.

A list of really complicated (read: horrendous! And with this statement I am *not* siding with any group as such) things happened on the borders between Israel and the Palestinian territories. It is no simple matter. In the midst of this horror story of suicide bombings and terrorist attacks, the state of Israel built a massive 13-meter high wall, dividing Jerusalem into Palestinian and Israeli areas. To understand the bottomless pit of contrasting views on this act of severing, one *has* to hear both narratives. And definitely not via the media.

Christy was once cornered by an extended family member, with a gun against her head, and threatened with death if she'd open her mouth again in support of the Biblical stance on ownership of the land. Shortly after this ordeal, a British couple visited their "House by the Wall" which at the time had already become a famous landmark for the supporters of the 'atrocities enacted against Palestinians'.

The British couple offered Christy political asylum in the UK and they found a way for her out of Bethlehem. They offered her lodging, education and a list of other perks in return for her account of the Israeli-Palestinian narrative.

When Christy and I had our Skype call, she had already been with Harold and his wife for around two years. She sounded confident about her life as a lobbyist, which entailed a lot of travelling and speaking.

Christy and I kept messaging each other two or three times a day for the duration of our tour. She later admitted to me that she was continuously testing whether or not I was sincere. And as the weeks progressed and our cycle tour was approaching its end in Jerusalem, matters with Christy's situation started heating up.

Our little cycling group aimed to reach Jerusalem in time for Emile and Jana's wedding. In the few weeks leading up to this, I tried several times to patch up my shattered relationship with Emile. To no avail. I offered to help them with the wedding music, but they amicably declined. The hurt it caused was severe.

Two days before their wedding, Christy asked me to visit her parents in Bethlehem. Bethlehem is situated about 10 kilometres south of Jerusalem. To get into Bethlehem one needs to pass through the Israeli security checkpoint. I cycled there while praying all the way. I had been in contact with Christy's folks for some time and this made the way slightly easier. The IDF soldier at the checkpoint was amused by my fully loaded bicycle and asked where I was heading.

"Anastas family."

"Welcome!" ... It felt like cycling into a post-apocalyptic arena where time was surely forgotten.

The Anastas family's home was exactly what I imagined: fenced-in on three sides by a massive stone-cold wall full of graffiti. The complexity besieging the house and its contextual setting felt like a thick blanket over the entire area. It felt spiritually messy.

I slowly and prayerfully pushed my bike downhill to the three-story house. Nobody in sight. I was in a bad movie scene.

Christy's mom, Claire, opened the front door. After so many weeks communicating with her daughter, the relief was palpable. It felt like Claire was my own flesh and blood. We hung out at the house for most of the day, sharing stories and tears. I stayed over in their huge empty guesthouse and we prayed together before I cycled back to Jerusalem the following afternoon.

What to make of it all?

Emile and Jana's Jerusalem wedding was beautiful beyond words! Most of our original *Shmitah* group was there, and the joys of being united again and sharing in the celebration overshadowed my feeling of despondency.

They had a fairy-tale reception under Israeli stars against the backdrop of the 500-year old walls of the Old City. We returned to our hostel, and in an instinctive way our small *Shmitah* group diverged that night.

I took a bus to Mizpe Ramon and spent a couple of much-needed days alone in the desert.

Two friends in South Africa knew about my journey with Christy and her family and encouraged and eventually supported me financially to fly to Christy in England. Before leaving for the UK, I visited Claire again and was faced with the Anastas family's concern about what was *really* going on with us. First there was a British man who 'took away' their daughter, and now a stranger from South Africa was about to fly to her… Claire trusted me on Christy's account, but I also believe there was a God-connection that she understood.

She sent a backpack full of Christy's clothes with me. At check-in at Ben Gurion Airport, a young security officer made me unpack all of Christy's clothes, shoes, perfume… "This yours?" … I smiled; we both blushed. "You can go!" And so, I departed once again for the UK, but this time my mission was discreet and only understood by a small minority.

Like Nico and Surita who welcomed me into their home in London. Nico and I went to primary school together until their family moved out of town. I had such a wonderful sense of safety when I saw Nico waiting for me at Gatwick Airport in freezing London. We drove back to their home, mulling over the why's, the what's and all the years gone by.

Christy and I scheduled to meet at Victoria Train Station. I had a small pack with me and was disguised behind balaclava and sunglasses... nervous to the core.

The only contact we had was via Skype and figuring out where to meet-up was quite tricky. But we eventually walked into each other in an obscure little alehouse, movie-scene style.

"You can take off your glasses. They know you're here," was basically our hello's. Meeting Christy in person was a spiritual moment for me. Not for any surreptitious agenda, but rather that *the* moment had its build-up for months. I remembered how my dad and I sat in Oudtshoorn watching her speak on YouTube, and here we sat facing each other.

Christy and I spoke for hours. We covered history and life and Israel and God, and everything in between. It really felt like we'd known each other for years. I also shared with her my adult-life tragedy with Michaela, and curiously she could relate on several points.

Over the course of three months we had been speaking with each other every single day. Obviously, there was a massive question mark hanging over our connection and me being there with her.

Nico and Surita took amazing care of me in the days that followed. I had no money, but they made sure I had shelter, food and train tickets. The two of them fully bought into my mission - whatever the outcome was supposed to be, I'm not sure!

Christy had to do a couple of talks over the course of the week, most of which I attended. I met Harold, and there was tension between us but probably only him and I were aware of it.

It was obvious that Christy wasn't at all free to do what she wanted. *Something* uneasy was lurking beneath the surface. I confronted the situation during one of our coffee dates and uncovered a serious plot. So much so, that I received a call from Harold, who at the time had told Christy that he was *very* uncomfortable with me around. He wanted to 'come see me in person' in Seven Oaks where I stayed with Nico and Surita.

We met up in a coffee shop. It was easy to spot what was really going on. Harold was collecting money from her speaking engagements as her "manager". But things were on his terms only. Christy had zero options but to oblige. She was not only a political refugee; she was very cleverly trapped. Some of the things which Harold relayed to me about Christy and their setup made me realise that there also wasn't much integrity that she could bank on. And in a trice, it dawned on me why I was 'sent' to London: to help Christy get out of her entrapment.

Christy soon resigned from Harold's organisation with nowhere to go. I was inspired by her boldness! That Friday evening before I returned to Israel, we invited Christy to a Shabbat meal at Nico's house. She arrived early and was viscerally distraught. "What's going on, Christy?"
"I am angry at God!" she responded.

Nico and Surita headed out to the grocery store, so Christy and I took a walk. "What happened...?" Christy then told me that when I shared my story about Michaela, she strongly started feeling that God might have been preparing me all along... to become her husband. And she really was *not* interested in me in that way.

"I am *so* mad at God right now..." It was an intense conversation right before Shabbat, but we left it at that.

Breaking bread and sharing wine that night was special. But the evening was loaded with emotion and when Christy left, I sensed that this chapter was far from over.

Nico took me to Gatwick Airport the next day and I headed straight back to Jerusalem where I joined my friends Hannes and Lieze for a part of their tour of the Land.

After a week I was back on my own again. At this point I was really low on resources. I might have had just enough *shekels* for one more night in the Abraham Hostel. Meanwhile, Christy and I were in constant communication as if the past couple of days in London were merely part of the script. She told me that her family desperately needed a couple of hundred shekels. As I was reading at breakfast the following day, an elderly Dutch lady walked up to me and pushed a roll of banknotes into my hand, "I saw you reading Bible this morning and felt to give this to you."

It was exactly the number of shekels I needed to give to the Anastas family, plus enough to pay for my lodging for the entire Feast of Tabernacles. I was again blown away by God's provision.

Christy and I didn't speak about that Shabbat night in London again, but there was something in the air that needed clarity. I was contemplating the very real possibility that Christy might be my future wife. During that Festival week in Jerusalem, a number of things lined up for me to visit Christy again.

I reached out to my friends Johann and Aritha who had set up a business in Malta to hear if Christy and I could come and visit them. After all, it would be quite a safe space to figure out relational stuff in the presence of a grounded, married couple! So, I arranged my flight to London and a trip for Christy and me to Malta.

I was nervous to see Christy again because we were now trying to probe whether romance was in this whole affair… My flight to London Gatwick was different than weeks earlier. I had tickets booked for us to Malta the following day. I remember getting to the airport and both of us went, "Nah… this is not going to become romantic…" Which was an icebreaker to our trip in and of itself.

Johann picked us up and tried his best not to ask directly what we were on about. We didn't know either! It was very insightful to stay with Johann and Aritha in their massive house. They had four kids at the time and their household ran on a strict regime.

I had no money in the bank and since the objective of our trip was to figure out whether or not God wanted us to get married, matters were not simple. We did a solo trip to the northern part of Malta, and *that* was a day of analysis, debating, dining, wining… and a *very* good kiss. But as far as I recall we went to bed that night convinced that we were not heading to the altar. We both realised that our friendship was meant for a completely different objective. Nonetheless, we enjoyed an exquisite 8-day holiday!

Upon our return to London, I spoke to my dad's doctor on the phone. He told me that my dad was really ill and that he'd come home had he been in my shoes. But my dad, who was an intrepid adventurer earlier in his life, urged me to come home only when my flight was due.

As I left Christy and London behind, I knew it was time to head back to my family. I had much to process after months of probing, praying, meeting Christy in person and eventually flying to an island together only to discover that our shared journey had a very different purpose than what we could make out from afar. Few people in this world I respect as much as Christy. She is a humble and powerful human because she keeps on keeping Yahweh at the centre. And the amazing report is that our journey continues to this day.

As I mentioned at the beginning of the chapter, the Hebrew *seventh* year is understood to be a year that contrasts significantly to the six that go before it.

During the *Shmitah* I tasted of the goodness of God through the deliverance from financial debt and provision through the kindness of friends and strangers in a way that this chapter could never do justice.

It is difficult to practice letting the ground rest. Most of us are not farmers, and the idea to stop working makes little or no sense in our modern lives. My proverbial piece of land was the music industry, and in the run-up to March 2014, I had spent all of my adult life striving and struggling to survive in it.

At times I wonder what would have happened to me had I not stopped and laid my feeble piece of earth to rest.

8

FALL OF ROME

*"I wasn't there that
morning when my father
passed away,
I didn't get to tell him
all the things I had to say..."*

- Mike + The Mechanics

5 February 2015.

I woke up around 06:30 with a phone call from my mother. When I answered and heard an unknown male voice, I *knew* it was over.

"Helmut, this is Doctor Vermeulen…" His voice was kind but deliberate.
"…is it dad?"
"Yes. Take it easy and come home when you can. There's nothing to rush now."

In a daze, I walked out of the guest room and bumped into my friend Retief's wife.
"Good morning! Did you sleep well?" she asked friendly and altogether oblivious. "Umm. Yes… I guess. My dad just died."

Ten years of battling with cancer had gotten the best of him.

Retief and his wife drove me to the airport within the hour, and I composed myself until I phoned my friend Hannes who also lost his dad, some years prior and then I broke down in tears in the airport lounge.

I arrived at my folks' home in Oudtshoorn late that night and remember my mother's anaemic frame when she opened the door that evening. I poured us wine and we sobbed and talked about dad for hours. It was healing but also debilitating.

I went to my mom's room to see if she was okay in the middle of the night. As I stood in the door watching her sleep alone in the bed on which my dad breathed out his last that very morning, my heart broke.

Everything about *that picture* was just so wrong.

Christmas 2014 was the last time we were together as a family. The atmosphere was one of brokenness, but we also had so much joy being together. My sister took stunning pictures of us all, and to this day one of them remains the profile pic of our family's *WhatsApp* group.

Dad was deteriorating rapidly after Christmas, to the point that I didn't want to leave my folks. But he encouraged me to continue with the music. I flew back to Cape Town via George and as I left the terminal building on my way to the plane, I received a phone call from my dad telling me that he was proud of me and that he'd do the same had he been in my shoes. I remember saying *goodbye* to him on the phone, more than once in that month, believing it was his last.

In the midst of a rollercoaster January, I left for Pretoria to start working on studio albums for both Retief Burger and Julanie J.

We were but a couple of days in, when I received the portentous phone call from our family doctor on the morning of February 5th. Life came to a halt for many weeks. Never to return to the normal I knew.

UNDERWORLD

The Ancient Hebrews did not understand where diseased ones went after their last breath. We don't know either. We have theology and philosophy to help us, but the truth is: it is a mystery.

The Hebrew word "SHE'OL" is understood as the *underworld* and is often translated as "grave" - the abode of the dead. But it's the verbal form "SHA'AL" that holds the clue. It literally means "to ask [where]".

This strange Hebrew concept began to make sense in the week that we had to deal with my dad's memorial service and cremation. I woke up many mornings (and more than often from daydreaming), and asked, "where *are* you!?" ... There are no dress rehearsals for this most liminal experience.

I visited the funeral services to pay for my dad's cremation, as well as for their assistance with the church service. Handing my credit card over to cashier that day, felt *simply* bizarre.

We had our last viewing of his body before the funeral. I went in first. Coffin, flowers, dimmed light, funeral music. My heart cramped as I stared in disbelief at his handsome but lifeless face. I remember going back in with my sister, and how her breakdown tore me apart. Again.

The memorial service was held in the church where he was the organist for many years. I compiled a few of his favourite Bach tracks - as per his last wish - which played as the people walked in. Many of our friends and family came to offer heartfelt support, all the way from Stellenbosch and even as far as Pretoria.

I sang "Sielemens", an Afrikaans song I wrote that became somewhat popular amongst Christian believers and then I attempted to offer a few words about his life at the end of the service. I am grateful to my mother who gave me an *Inderal* to drink. 'Out of body experience' is an understatement!

It was almost mid-point between two successive sabbatical years, so I had the privilege to be with my mother for weeks at a time. Most strangely, there was always money in the bank. I didn't own a car at the time, and my conviction was not to charge money for production work, but through the *chuppah* (covering) of our new company, StoneBear & Mayor, everything somehow worked out well.

I did *not* process my dad's passing away. I didn't know how to do it. It was, and to some extent it remains a deep, dark pit plastered with emotional hieroglyphs.

One morning as I was reading outside my mom's humble abode, a small bird landed on the table. I noticed from his awkward landing that his one foot was completely broken off. He was hopping on one little claw and one stump. And *right there* I broke down in a sob. I went for a run in the hills to try to pull myself together, but I couldn't stop crying. The helplessness of that little creature cracked open the vault suppressing my own sense of loss.

I wrote a song that day called 'Little Bird' which I made a demo of but never finished.

> "Little bird,
> why did you come here?
>
> Little bird, you remind me
> we all fly
>
> I watch as you disguise,
> you are hurting
>
> Little bird, you remind me…
> we all die."

JUBILEE

The Jubilee commenced in March 2015. In many ways this year and what it means is one of the most obscure concepts in the Bible, perhaps because it only happens once in most of our lifetimes. I really wanted to understand the Jubilee's significance. As a 37-year old, I knew I probably had one chance of experiencing it.

Leviticus 25:10-14 (WEB) reads:

> "You set the fiftieth year apart,
> and proclaim liberty throughout the land
> to all its inhabitants.

> *It is to be a Jubilee to you;*
> *and each of you shall return to*
> *your own property,*
> *and each of you shall return to his family."*

> *"That fiftieth year shall be a Jubilee to you.*
> *In it you do not sow,*
> *neither reap that which grows of itself,*
> *nor gather from the undressed vines."*

> *"...it shall be holy to you.*
> *You shall eat of its increase out of the field."*

> *"...each of you shall return to his property."*

> *"If you sell anything to your neighbour,*
> *or buy from your neighbour,*
> *you shall not wrong one another."*

This fiftieth year, which is said to be treated as *holy* (in Hebrew this word means to "set apart" or "have a different purpose"), is all about liberty, property and family.

"Proclaim *liberty* throughout the *land*" ... "return to your own *property* and... *family.*"

The Jewish sages say that the Jubilee is really *all* about the land: a physical return to, or restoration unto the original owners. What a strange and beautiful concept! It does not take special insight to realise that the objective of such an amazing year is about releasing people from debt, reuniting families and returning *rightful* ownership to land.

For me and a handful of friends who decided to explore the Jubilee concept, it was nothing short of crazy to commit ourselves to a second sabbatical year. And even more so for me after losing my dad mid-point between these two consecutive and obscure years.

I was convinced - even right up to the end of the Jubilee - that something significant (for example like a victory for land) was going to happen in Israel. But nothing obvious happened on the world stage.

STONEBEAR & MAYOR

During our *Shmitah* in Israel, I grappled with the idea of offering my music production services for free. The idea simply would not let go of me.

At the time I drafted an email to about twenty of my favourite clients offering to produce two albums free of charge, first come first serve. Since I had almost no studio equipment left, whoever would jump at the invitation would simply need to hire a studio for the process. Two artists responded.

But it wasn't until about a month later in London when I received an interesting email from Lukas de Beer. Lukas' Afrikaans album "Storm op Jupiter" was the last record I made in 2013 before leaving for the *Shmitah*.

When Lukas emailed me his proposal - that the two of us start a joint venture together - I was reminded of an incident back in 2013: when he made his studio booking, he paid a lump sum - much more than the required booking fee and also months in advance - simply to make sure his slot was secure. *This* small gesture communicated trust. In the email from Lukas he suggested that he will put down cash so we could buy back all of my old studio equipment and also acquire whatever else we would need additionally.

Around mid-December that year *StoneBear & Mayor Records* was born. Effortlessly.

Our first project was an Afrikaans single for William Loedolff, leader of the band *G.L.O*, with a title translated to "It is Done". I remember how I final-mixed the song in the room adjacent to my bedridden dad. When I listen to the song now, I can still hear his oxygen machine woven into the fabric of the music.

SLIPPED DISC

In July 2015 I decided to visit my mother by cycling the R62 for four days, from Stellenbosch to Oudtshoorn. It sounded like a great adventure, the weather looked good, and… it was the Jubilee!

I didn't tell my mom, but my sister knew about my little trip.

Moral of the story: one shouldn't try to cycle around a 100 kilometres per day with a fully loaded bicycle, not having done any of that in months. But I made it from Stellenbosch over the Franschhoek pass to the Theewaterskloof Dam on the first day. Splendid low light winter scenery camping next to the water.

The following day I cycled to Montagu breaking my body over the course of 110 kilometres. I spent a great night at the famous *De Bos* campsite. But the following morning my legs were throbbing with pain. When I got back on my bike, I knew that two massive passes between Montagu and Warmwaterberg (a hot spring in the middle of the Karoo), awaited me.

By lunchtime I made it to the top of the first pass.
I was broken.

By that time, I could barely walk. I decided to perform a little stretch-maintenance sequence when I heard an audible laceration of my hamstring. Big trouble!

I rode down the mountain pretending this injury didn't happen. I struggle to remember how I actually made it all the way to Barrydale. From there I hitch-hiked to Warmwaterberg and spent hours in the hot pools with the hope of sorting out my limping legs.

The next morning, I could manage a slow cycle to reach Ladismith. But that was as far as my body would go. I phoned my mother. She was elated to hear my voice, but she was *not* happy about my cycling attempt. The drive to

Ladismith was her *first* solo cruise without my dad, but she made it and appreciated my little surprise visit to Oudtshoorn.

But there was one small problem: over the course of the days that followed my stiffness slowly but surely morphed into… a *slipped disc!* This was not my first episode of lower back issues, and it wasn't even nearly as acute as my first experience of it in 2012, but I was barely able to walk for almost 8 weeks thereafter. By September I had gained enough confidence to start jogging again.

Then came the *real* surprise.

At first, I thought, "…whoa, I'm really unfit!" But the pain in my chest simply wouldn't recede. Some days were better than others, but on most days the pressure was so severe that I could barely do 100 metres before needing to stop and clasp my chest. "What on earth was going on…!?"

This continued for weeks.

During this time, I was approached by the fashion consortium *TFG* to compose a second theme song for them. The project miraculously took me less than a week to wrap up and earned me enough money to buy an Audi Allroad, cash. This is possibly one of the cars I coveted the most and I could hardly believe the grace I was shown to drive one for several years.

CARI QUOYESER

I met Cari in the small desert town of *Mitzpe Ramon* in Israel the year before. She was a volunteer at the Green Backpackers Hostel where I stayed for one night. We barely spoke, but about a week later we bumped into each other again at the Abraham's Hostel in Jerusalem. I was introverting away with a glass of house wine at a small table in the lounge area. We recognised each other and she joined me. "So, tell me your story?" I asked her.

"Well... I am a singer-songwriter from Texas, on a sabbatical in Israel. And you?" I chuckled in disbelief, "No ways! I am a music producer from South Africa... *also* on a sabbatical in Israel."

The night transformed into storytelling and exchanging our tales. It felt like we had a timeless connection. Cari told me that she will perform at the hostel's 'open mic night' the following evening. Wow, she owned the stage and mesmerised the audience with so much musical prowess and boldness. We decided to work together there and then.

StoneBear had very little to offer other than swagger and time, but Cari decided to take the risk and come visit us in Stellenbosch. We would take care of her costs in South Africa, if she would take care of her flight. Together we explored a bit of songwriting, but we really hoped for at least one strong single to emerge from her two weeks in Cape Town.

One day Cari and I went for an afternoon hike-run to our local landmark, "Eerste Baken" ('First Beacon'). On the way up, I felt the same tightness of chest. I had to stop more than once to recalibrate. Strangely the pain would subside somewhat after a decent pause. We made it to First Beacon and back home before sunset.

We were going to have dinner and continue working on Cari's music when a little accident happened. As I was reaching for my towel on the washing line, I knocked my head on the edge of the steel electricity box. I could hear the metal crashing into my skull. In a reflex, I grabbed at my forehead, but the blood was already gushing over my face. I called out for help and within minutes we were rushing to the hospital - me with a towel on my head to try and stem the bleeding.

The emergency personnel were incredible. The doctor-on-call wasted no time before he stitched the burst artery and stopped the bleeding. He then continued with a list of routine checks, and as I lay there in complete incredulity, the pathology lady came to me with a vial of my blood in her hand.

"Uhm. When last have you had your cholesterol checked, sir?" she asked in a matriarchal tone.
"I can actually *see* the problem in your blood…"

I rang my dear friend Pierre Tredoux. He was our drummer for Merchant Seal back at varsity days and was now one of *the* most rated internist specialists in the area.

Pierre immediately connected the dots between my chest pain and the miracle accident that got me to the pathologist in E.R. And thanks to Pierre's network of doctor friends, I was scheduled for an angiogram within a couple of days.

But Cari was still with us and on a very tight time schedule on a trip that cost her a fortune. I was ridden with angst and confusion as to why this was happening, but on doctor's orders, I was removed from all music-making endeavours.

The evening prior to my medical procedure at Tygerberg Hospital, Cari and I stayed at a luxury apartment on Clifton beach. She was very upset with me that night. Her own father has had several angiograms… and here she was ambuscaded into all of it again.

ANGIOGRAM

The angiogram procedure took about 45 minutes. I lay strapped and semi-drugged with both arms in different directions and overheard in detail the cardiologist's quandary over my wrecked coronary artery network. I was befuddled with anxiety, and *with* an overbearing sense of responsibility for Cari's visit, my mother being alone in Oudtshoorn, my dad had passed away… and to top matters: I had no medical aid!

I don't wish upon my enemies the perplexity of those couple of days in and out of the hospital.

Lukas took the situation with Cari in his stride and while I was in the hospital, they wrote an amazing song called "War". Today it lies truncated yet brimming with commercial potential.

I went home and to my astonishment and thanks to my friend Pierre, the angiogram and hospitalisation didn't cost me a cent! Well, … I had to pay an administration fee of less than a 100 Rand. Surreal.

Our last couple of days with Cari allowed us to finalise her song "Fall of Rome". On a number of levels, my physical falling apart - half-way through the Jubilee - was profoundly marked by Cari's visit and this single which spoke viscerally to an issue I wouldn't see for years to come.

I cautiously took to the trails again.

But the pain in my chest did *not* go away.

9

STRONG

*"I don't know how we made it this way
We left not seeing beyond the fray
Never meant to be whom I was the first day
I think we made it here to stay."*

- Calev

My singular dream since I began making music in the 90s was to write and perform my own songs. Not many people know this. And very few of my close friends know how difficult it is (and will always be) for a music producer to become a performing artist. Only a marginal few ever make it.

I am not one of them.

Yet the journey leading up to my first solo project, *Calev*, had significant twists and turns.

Tygerberg Hospital, March 2016.

I tried to convince myself to believe that I was getting better. But nearly six months later I was *back* on the treadmill in the Cardiology Unit.

The ECG was not going to lie: the first angiogram did not really make any difference to the discomfort in my chest.

There was one difference though. In those months I had written seven songs for my *Calev* project. As much as the dreaded Coronary Artery Disease was still looming, the recording of my solo project was well underway!

CALEV

The Hebrew word "CALEV" literally means 'dog'. Constructed from the words "KOL" (meaning 'all') and "LEV" ('heart'), *Calev* also literally means 'all heart' or 'whole heart' - which is exactly the ancient understanding of a dog.

Caleb (or Calev) in the Bible is mentioned in Numbers 24:14 as a man who "had a different spirit with him and has followed [Yahweh] fully." I have *always* related to this obscure Biblical figure - for his ardour on the one end, but even more so for his curious decree recorded in Joshua 14:10-11:

"Now, behold, Yahweh has kept me alive,
as He spoke, these forty-five years,
from the time that Yahweh spoke this word to Moses,
while Israel walked in the wilderness:
and now, behold, I am this day eighty-five years old.

As yet I am as strong this day as in the day
that Moses sent me:
as my strength was then, even so is my strength now,
for war, and to go out and to come in."

Calev as a project was born on the same treadmill of the Cardiology Unit, just six months earlier. I still recall the voice inside, "What *more* needs to happen for you to choose the music inside of you?" I was arrested by the thought. Not because it was completely novel, but rather because my denial of so many years had finally caught up with me.

And in that moment of truth, I decided to matter.

I put out the word to a handful of friends and family about my dream to record an album of my own. Two of my friends immediately reached out with an offer to invest in the project. I began writing without hesitation and remember those endless December nights behind the piano and just how difficult it was to snap out of the 'helping others' mode.

Inspired by several of my muses - Coldplay, Enigma, A-Ha - I wrote a list of songs, most of which were thrown out after a verse or hook or idea. But seven songs made the list. I decided to stick with them and to call the album "Break the Silence". Which is still quite apt.

I started recording *Calev* with my close compadres Sven Blumer (on guitars), Iwan Kemp (on drums) and my colleague Lukas (on bass). By the time I had my second angiogram in March, we had progressed well, and the dream of releasing a first solo project was slowly but surely turning into a reality.

SECOND ANGIOGRAM

I was exceptionally nervous that the second procedure would also not be fully successful. But the beautiful assurance that much of my *Calev* journey was about being strong at 85, made everything feel simpler.

The angiogram procedure felt much longer than the first time, and again I overheard the cardiologists discussing my curious arterial situation. At the end of the procedure, the doctor related casually that he hoped I was much better after this, since there wasn't much else they could do to intervene!

"Tomorrow morning when you're up, go and run! As fast as you can. You need blood through this system."

And oh, the inexpressible joy as I darted all along the Sea Point Promenade the next morning… the pain was *gone*!

My daily routine then comprised of drinking lots of freshly squeezed juices (and lots of red wine with my flatmate Etienne), working on *Calev* and running around in the mountains. After months of angina, the relief from pain was beyond words.

Calev was officially launched at the Bellingham Cellar outside Franschhoek on August 28. The evening was a stylish event of wine, canapés, a live recording of our songs and the hope that it would be *the* beginning of the journey I had dreamt of most of my life. In the weeks and months that followed I ploughed an endless amount of energy into marketing *Calev* as a live performance act. But very little came of the effort. I ran into a brick wall.

While sifting and sorting through much chaos in my heart (excuse the pun), living near the Sea Point Promenade added a layer of rest and restoration which helped to process the many open tabs in my life.

Towards the latter part of 2016, I began recording music for other people again. The dream of singing and performing on my own slowly started to die. I tried everything to make Calev work.

But there was nothing.

I moved back to Stellenbosch to reopen my little music production hub with my former colleagues, and ended up working hours upon hours every day, merely to afford rent. Nothing about that made any sense. I deeply resented the full circle which had me trapped. All over again.

Etienne and I rented a house in Stellenbosch, both just needing a lock-up-and-go. I recall half-way through 2017 how I felt like I was back in sophisticated slavery but at least I had a 65-kilometre *Fish River Canyon Ultra Marathon* to look forward to. I was happy with my progress in training. But on the day of the race in July, and following a sleepless night, I suffered an upset stomach and due to dehydration could not finish the race. At 43 kilometres - shivering and spastic - the medics pulled me out and put me on a drip. I had to watch my friend and teammate Daniel scuttle off into the distance and finish the race without me. I was super proud of him! My personal disappointed would have been contained had my heart been less vulnerable but I felt stumped.

John Eldridge writes in his book "Wild At Heart" about a sea lion. Left in the wrong place for too long this metaphor implies that we also come to think of *that* wrong place as 'home'. The remainder of 2017 embodied that sadness for me. I taught Biblical Hebrew, hung out with amazing people, continued running, travelled to Israel for the Biblical

Feasts... but something in me was restless and seeking a way out.

Towards the end of 2017, I decided to pause our music hub and take to the road. I knew I needed a break from everything that added to the pressure.

I left Stellenbosch with my fully loaded SUV: camping gear, off-road tackle, recording equipment... the works. I drove to Hermanus in search of my lost nomadic self and felt... free. That evening a bunch of friends celebrated a new year's evening with a jolly gathering on a wine farm.

And then an unexpected reunion.

Chantelle and I first met in 2013 at a social gathering where I stuck out like a sore finger in a house full of close compatriots. Chantelle also stood out... in appearance.

We immediately struck a chord speaking about the Myers Briggs personality types. When I left that evening the friend who invited me warned me sternly. "That girl will break your heart."

More or less three years passed. One night at a mutual friend's birthday party, Chantelle and I ended up next to each other and spent two hours talking about personality types again. I thoroughly enjoyed her mind, and I tried to persuade her to visit us in Sea Point. This never realised. Not even the jacuzzi on our balcony helped.

Another year passed, and out of the blue, one afternoon while doing my usual run in Jonkershoek, Chantelle phoned me. She wanted to sell me some or other financial product, to which my response was, "I have my fingers in several pies. So… thank you, but I'm not interested right now!"

She thought that my running in the mountains sounded like an opportunity for us to do some jogging together. Many more months and several half-hearted invitations of spending time together passed. This confirmed my friend's warning. But I set an ultimatum for myself for *that* new year's evening on the wine farm.

Chantelle and I began spending a lot of time together after our reunion - mostly under the auspice of running in the mountains and having wine or bubbly afterwards. And by the end of January, summer and hormones landed us in a relationship!

But! I had already decided to remain nomadic… A decision that we - no, I - messed up royally. At first, I managed to house-sit a friend's place and later ended up staying wherever I could find a quiet enough space to produce tracks for clients on the fly. My fantasy of travelling around and investing time and energy into my songs, fell by the wayside. And all of this in the name of love!

Chantelle and I are high-energy humans! And we have complimentary personality styles on most levels. But on several crucial points, I was embarking on a mission that I could never see through.

We had endless fun and adventures. *And* we had drama. Which was fun and funny in the beginning. But I realised soon that our kindred and amicable personality styles had a dark side. At least for me.

It also dawned on me that what I had promised myself for that year, was not going according to plan. In May I set off for a recording project with my friend Sanet Lambrechts in Namibia. The idea was to road trip all the way to their farm, camping along the way and making music wherever facilities allowed. The trip was a good palette cleanser and gave me enough time to ponder my nomadic life and the added pressures of a relationship that was either going to end, or miraculously turn into marriage.

I was unaware of the emotional stress I was enduring at the time... until my old Audi Allroad broke down more than once in the middle of the Namibian desert, on the way back to South Africa.

I was driving along the C24 - a very bad gravel road between the desert and Rehoboth, with zero mobile phone reception - when I tore my rear left tyre. And of course, I only had but a ridiculous biscuit as a spare wheel. I waited and prayed for about an hour for a car to pass. Stopping an old gentleman, I begged him to get help from the police in Rehoboth. Nothing came from that. After another half an hour, a truck with two young men pulled over and offered to get my torn tyre fixed in Rehoboth. I was stranded about 10 kilometres out of town. The two lads told me that they needed about an hour, and as they drove off with my wheel it dawned on me that I didn't even ask their names. Let alone their phone numbers.

Hours passed. By sunset I started feeling very ill. I had been struggling with an ulcer for quite some time, but *that* Saturday afternoon I was not okay. Just as I was about to cave in, the two guys reappeared on the scene with a replaced tyre which took them hours to find and a lot of money! I was broken as much as I was overwhelmed by their kindness. Following them to an ATM in Rehoboth, I broke down sobbing. And there and then I decided to head straight back home. It was a full day's driving to the Namibian border. I arrived in the small town of Springbok and put my car on Gumtree, right away.

My fortieth was on the 29th of May 2018. About 80 friends and family gathered at an eatery. It was a magical evening of good food, wine, cigars, speeches... the works. But that night, I was without a car or house or any form of predictable income. I did *not* imagine this for my life on a milestone birthday.

At the end of June, I moved into a beautifully restored Cape Dutch house on the farm 'By Den Weg' - which translates to "on the way" or "by the wayside".

My mom moved in with me. As did my friend and guitarist Sven. And Chantelle's best friend, Ziggy - who at the time did *not* appreciate me.

Moving in together sounded like a feasible idea: it was a *big* house, Lukas and I loved our new studio space, we were *in* the vineyards, and Chantelle and I had all the more reason to hang out together at our place... But pressure on all levels was about to increase.

It was not a cheap homestead. It was also complicated for relational dynamics. Lukas and I slogged away for hours on a project for a digital TV station, for very little income - all in the name of school fees! Chantelle's imminent vocation as a Financial Advisor also added to the complexity. We had drama on one too many levels.

On the one end, we were living the dream, but on the other end, I found myself spun into a web of aggrieved personal decisions, a relationship that I wanted to end, drama upon drama between housemates, my mother, our landlord... and all of that set against mounting financial pressure.

Towards the end of winter, I went out for my usual late afternoon trod in the hills in some of the most beautiful natural scenery around Stellenbosch. I started itching weirdly about ten minutes into my run. The intensity of this escalated quickly and I phoned Chantelle to prepare me a hot bath. She recognised from my symptoms that something more serious might be wrong and told me to head home immediately.

On my run down the hill, the itching became so acute that I started feeling light-headed. I crashed to the ground right in front of our house. Long story short: four of us in the car, Chantelle chased me to hospital, speeding through a roadblock while my mother prayed out loud for my survival. I could not breathe anymore by the time they dragged me into the E.R... According to the doctor, my life was saved by minutes. To this day we don't know what caused the anaphylaxis, but it sure woke me up to the emotional discord and burned-out state I was in.

About a week later Chantelle and I ended our relationship. I couldn't carry on. But we *did* go to Israel together as if nothing was wrong.

My strange romantic relationship with Chantelle triggered aspects of my heart that I knew nothing of before our journey together. We are still amazing friends. I can attest that she is one of the most warm-hearted and sincere humans that I know, love and respect. But I also realised my deep-seated ailment from which I needed rescue.

After five weeks in Israel I came home refreshed. Chantelle and I tried another relational round for a couple of weeks. But again - I simply couldn't.

That December, my friend Etienne instigated a conversation with me about personal boundaries and 'fairness to self'. I recall being solo at a fire one night, realising that being fair to self - on both a transactional and transformational level - is a skill to acquire when you are young. Not at forty.

10

GAZE

*"People do not decide their futures.
They decide their habits,
and their habits decide their futures."*

- F.M. Alexander

Very few things truly worthwhile happen swiftly.

This is what the Ancients understood intuitively.

The Christian view on 'worship' is far more inspired by Greek philosophy than Ancient Hebrew understanding. Contrary to what we've been taught, both the concepts 'praise' and 'worship' have nothing intrinsically to do with music.

I am not saying that music does not play a fascinating or even important role, *or* that the Bible does not prompt us to make music and sing [new] songs unto Yahweh. But let's focus on the language.

In Hebrew (as in Greek) several ancient words often get translated into the same English word. The English word 'praise' is a prime example of this.

The most common Hebrew verb translated as 'to praise' is the word "HALAL". The parent root of this word is the noun "HAL", which consists of the letters "HEH" (a picture of a man pointing something out) and "LAMED" (a shepherd's staff) and could mean 'look, the leader'. This word "HAL" also means 'the north star'. The Ancients considered the north star as the 'fixed point' or 'leader' in the skies which they employed and relied upon for their orientation in the desert.

Can you see it? No pun intended. The concept behind the Hebrew word for 'praise' is to 'behold the leader'... 'to fix your eyes on the shepherd'.

One of *the* most used expressions in Christian doxology is the word "HALLELUYAH". The verbal root being… "HALAL".

Hallelu'Yah literally means 'We fix our gaze on Yah'. This changes everything. Long before our lyrics or our inspiring musical arrangements, before our bands and our stages - praising Yahweh was *all* about fixing our eyesight; fixating our gaze on Him!

The next word "SHACHAH" is usually translated as 'to worship'. This is a fascinating one. This verb is employed in the Biblical text for both man and God, and also for actions performed by man, unto both man and God.

When the verb is employed for an action performed by a human unto another human, the translators usually use phrases like 'do obeisance' or 'bow prostrate before'. And when the verb is employed for an action performed by a human unto God, they almost exclusively use the English word 'worship'.

The reader could miss out on the depth of the underlying Hebrew.

The verb "SHACHAH" literally means 'to bow down before…' The word is comprised of three Hebrew letters: a "SHIN" (picture of a tooth), a "CHET" (picture of a wall or barrier) and again a "HEH".

Put together, these three letters spell out something like 'to cut off the barrier of seeing'. The Ancients understood the action of bowing down before someone as pivotal to perceiving the other person correctly. Bowing down to a human implies respecting them for their intrinsic worth or value. And bowing before Yahweh means exactly the same!

Thus, both the English concepts of 'praise' and 'worship' have everything to do with our vision. I want to put it bluntly: our worship and laudation of God have everything to do with how we view God.

If we go one step further: how we see the world is how we see God is how we see everything ... and *this* is the point.

NETHERLANDS

I have known my friend André van Zyl from University days. He studied Dentistry and we met one night when our band Merchant Seal performed on the medical campus.

We immediately struck a friendly chord and years down the line when our lives had taken different turnoffs, he messaged me about recording an EP (short for "Extended Play" - usually four to six tracks, and a term dating from the vinyl era).

I was elated because at the time I had just returned from England and 'trying-to-make-it-in-Europe' didn't really work out.

We made a beautiful and edgy EP and in the years that followed I had the privilege of producing several live albums and other smaller projects for him.

When André called me in 2019 about the prospect of recording a studio album together later that year, I said yes! I suggested that I come to the Netherlands to produce the songs on his home turf.

I was at the airport about to depart, overloaded with recording gear, camping gear and all sorts of gimmicks to mix work and play (comma omitted intentionally!), when I received an emergency phone call from the security company looking after our farmhouse. A planned attack on several farms in the vicinity had leaked out. My mother was alone at home, and before boarding the plane, I guided her to safety over the phone.

In a strange way, that incident would frame the seven weeks that followed.

I rented a car in Amsterdam and visited my cousin and his wife in the beautiful village of Papendrecht. The following day Michaela arrived from Paris and we spent an innocent weekend in and around Amsterdam. Deep conversations, strolling the streets and visiting parks - we had lunches and dinners and made nothing more of it than an amicable catch-up.

I began working on André's twelve-track album "Gaze" from the solitude of their loft space. From the window, I had a view over the lush green countryside, but most of the days were typical greyed-out Dutch weather. I worked with headphones only. After the three weeks this added a surreal dimension to the album. Our daily rhythm included discussing the direction for a new song, and when André left for work, I'd jump in and spend hours sculpting musical parts.

But the strangest thing happened to me one morning as I went up to the loft, fresh cup of coffee in hand and ready to roll for the day. Out of nowhere, I suddenly had the notion popping up in my mind that *this* album was going to be my last. I couldn't even interpret the thought as making music for others was all I knew. This was how I stayed alive and looked after my mother financially...

We continued our daily music-making, and the record took shape. At the end of most days, I went for either a long bike ride or run. But I could not shake the thought that 'this is the end'.

Meanwhile, my relationship with my landlord back home deteriorated and I was *under pressure* to find an alternative stay for my mother.

André and I finished all our recordings for "Gaze" in about three weeks and I departed for an adventure-and-mixing-holiday on the Faroe Islands.

FAROE ISLANDS

My heart was racing as Atlantic Airways flight RC 456 from Copenhagen slowly descended between sheer-edged cliffs and over gaudy waters below.

Sørvágur Airport depicted otherworldliness. But I felt travel-fit and took my search for belonging elsewhere in my stride. My first impressions of the Faroe Islands included a mixture of raw and ridiculous beauty and super expensive *everything*. I took a taxi from the airport on the island of Vágar to the capital town of Tórshavn on the neighbouring island of Streymoy.

The greater Faroe Islands is an autonomous territory within the Kingdom of Denmark consisting of an archipelago of 18 major islands, situated between the Norwegian Sea and North Atlantic Ocean, at more or less equal distances from Scotland, Iceland and Norway.

Except for the two main islands which are ferry trips apart, all islands are connected via bridges or undersea tunnels, and the scenery is nothing short of unreal in every visceral sense. I have personally never experienced such beauty. Neither could I imagine a place so cold and perpetually rainy!

I wanted to visit the Faroe Islands on my own because I *had* to mix the "Gaze" album somewhere. I couldn't imagine a more inspiring place.

I spent one night in Tórshavn before grabbing a ferry to the southernmost island of Suðuroy the next day. In the aftermath of three weeks of relentless music-making, the night's rest in the local campsite - stormy as it was - was magical.

The two-hour ferry ride from Tórshavn to Suðuroy the following day felt surreal: deep blue North Atlantic waters with jagged islets as far as the eyes could see. I had an Airbnb booking on the island of Suðuroy for eight nights. From the description and pictures, it seemed perfect.

But as the ferry pulled into the harbour around 18:00 that day, I opened my Mac for one last time to double-check the address and phone number of my host. And then I saw that the host had cancelled my booking. The passengers were already disembarking, but I managed to get online with the Airbnb chat assistance. They were apologising profusely for the mishap. This made me realise that something went seriously wrong on my host's side that Airbnb could not be transparent about.

They reimbursed me immediately with an additional percentage! The only problem was it was already getting dark, and accommodation in that part of the woods is *not* that readily available.

I tried several times to phone my host, but her response was blunt, and I had no choice but to catch the last ferry of the day back to Tórshavn. At least I knew there was a campsite.

During the return journey on the ferry, I booked a single room in an Airbnb house on the outskirts of Tórshavn, and I decided that this change of plans was probably going turn into a good story.

I camped in stormy weather for another two nights, and luckily found a tiny shop near the harbour that rented out electric bikes. Now if there is *one* thing I would suggest to any traveller visiting the Faroe Islands, it would be to discover the island by e-bike. The country roads are relatively quiet, but the incredibly beautiful scenery changes every few minutes. And contrary to what you'd expect, the Faroe Islands are massive!

E-biking all over the Faroe Islands was the best fun ever, and I managed to cover hundreds of kilometres over the days that followed. When I took the ferry back to Suðuroy island, I had done almost 100 kilometres of exploration that day.

I shared the small Airbnb apartment with a Danish lady who happened to be as crazy as me. She was also a solo traveller and a radical adventure racer. As a result, I have to admit that my sense of competition pushed my physical limits a little further than planned.

One afternoon I took a break from a long mixing session behind my laptop and went for a run down the hill to buy provisions for the night. I wasn't even running hard but suddenly... the pain in my chest was back.

I remember pausing in complete disbelief, trying to compose myself... but realising that something was not okay. Again. And *that* after all the running and cycling of the past few weeks.

That evening I messaged my doctor and he handled the situation with so much wisdom. "Helmut, relax, try to enjoy your holiday and come see me when you're back."

SLÆTTARATINDUR

At 880 meters above sea level, Slættaratindur is the highest point on the Faroe Islands. I embarked on another adventure but knew that my heart was suffering. I also knew that it wasn't caused by my diet or medication or genetics.

Something else was at play.

My name means 'brave and assertive' in German. More than I would admit, this motivated me to embark on another full day of cycling and climbing.

I left Tórshavn at sunrise, taking my e-bike on a public bus to the village of Eiði located on the north-west tip of the island of Eysturoy. Wasting no time, I began pedalling up the steep and winding pass to the starting point of Slættaratindur.

It probably makes no sense to explain the anxiety one faces when you know your heart is not functioning well. But I leaned into that fear and uncertainty, left my bike there and raced up the highest mountain on the Faroe Islands, almost ceremonially.

With every step I felt less confident although the adrenaline was incredible!

I made it to the top! Slættaratindur was covered in clouds but for a moment the mist cleared up and I could see into eternity.

It was freezing cold and I had little time to linger. Going down the iconic mountain of the Faroe Islands transported me back to the reckless days we ran up and down the mountains of Stellenbosch. It took me another half a day of cycling in the rain to finally return to my humble abode in Tórshavn.

I completed the mixing and editing of "Gaze". In the week that followed, a series of flights and train rides took me to Paris and Cluj-Napoca (in Romania) and back to the Netherlands. I did some Masterclass work for clients in Romania and some more mixing on "Gaze" in France. I saw Michaela two more times, which always has a spiritual dimension to it.

On July the 3rd I travelled home - whatever was left of the concept - to a space that would never be the same again: neither physically nor metaphysically.

I was back at the Cardiac Unit and cycled courageously on the ECG bike as my friend Pierre again handled a dire situation with emotional intelligence. We laughed about old times and talked about Peter Gabriel and the boys, but when it came to the serious stuff, he did not spare me.

"Helmut, good and bad news. The good news is you will live; the bad news is you will have to stop producing music. Stress produces ulcers in some, and depression in others… but in your case, your heart is broken. You will have to find another way to make a living."

These were Pierre's words paraphrased. They were also the words that changed the direction and intentionality of everything in my life from that moment forward.

On August 1st, 2019 I had my third coronary artery intervention.

Doctor Helmut Weich captained the ship again, and three things transpired during that strange day:

Firstly, as I was lying all strapped up and drugged, I knew intrinsically that this would be my last angiogram. Writing this takes a lot of courage.

Secondly, I recall the screenshot of my coronary arterial network. Three years prior, that same screenshot looked dire beyond repair. Now I could see that the first two interventions were successful in arteries they unclogged. Hope was winning…

Thirdly - and this happened as I was driving home the following day - I sensed that YHWH wanted me to tell my story. I knew I had to write a book about how God systematically intervenes and gives us second chances.

By the time I reached my friends' home that day, some sort of table of contents had already taken shape in my mind.

And that is how "Fractal" began.

11

HARD TO HEART

"Tenderness is a deeper instinct than seduction, which is why it is so hard to give up hope."

- Michel Houellebecq

What do I make of my story of a broken heart?

Our journeys' passages are about returning our hearts to a tender and malleable state.

Yahweh God relentlessly invites us on this journey, and in our response, He redirects us back to Himself…

My years and years of obsession with Michaela, and the subsequent inability to deeply commit myself to any woman, coupled with my disappointment as an artist, shaped the journey of my own heart.

But essentially, I needed to discover that we are interconnected beings who need wholeness in every dimension of our lives.

A broken heart is *not* an abstract concept.

HEBRAIC PERSPECTIVE

If there is *one* thing that I have learned over the last decade while living with the dissonance of an increasing Hebrew worldview and at the same time quintessentially surviving in a Greek-thinking society, it's this:

We miss out on the depth of matters when our experiences are limited to the cognitive.

For example, it is one thing to have a thought-provoking discussion about how the original Saturday Sabbath turned into a Sunday-church-going-day but it's a completely different matter when we allow ourselves to be immersed in the real-life experience called *Shabbat.*

A couch traveller's approach to any concept (and I am reminded of the brilliant "The Art of Travel" by Alain de Botton) is simply incomparable to the real deal.

And yes, with the real deal we also face all the ubiquitous realities. But we simply cannot talk about concepts without immersing ourselves into them.

Nothing about the Hebrew worldview makes sense on paper. Take for example the *Shmitah* year: how do you decide *not* to plant or harvest? How do you *not* work? But immersing myself into it and giving up everything to experience it - *that* is what made all the difference.

Even though I could in no way afford to take off an entire year, I did. And walked away debt-free and transformed. This would make no sense in any realm but especially not in the close-circuit realm of the cognitive.

Part of the reason I decided to write this book is that I am witness to the transformational power of deep-diving into God's invitation, as opposed to merely entertaining the idea about it.

In the Gospels, we have a beautiful example when Yeshua appears before Pontius Pilate prior to His crucifixion. The various New Testament writers emphasise the dialogue between them slightly differently, but one thing transpires:

Pilate asks Yeshua a number of questions. Yeshua responds in true non-Greek fashion, and Pilate, in turn, asks more questions, related merely to the cognitive. When Yeshua answers Pilate's question regarding his Kingship, He tells him, "You say that I am a king. For this reason, I had been born, and for this reason I have come into the world, that I should testify to the *truth*. Everyone who is of the *truth* listens to my voice."

And then Pilate responds, "What is truth?"

At this point Yeshua keeps quiet. At this critical moment their dialogue had become irreconcilable. Because Pilate could not hear that Yeshua Himself was *the* Truth.

The Hebrew word for 'truth' is "EMET". This concept means 'glue of the covenant'. Yeshua was telling Pilate that He Himself was the bond between the Jewish people and Yahweh's covenant.

And *that* was beyond Pilate's worldview.

HEART TO HEART

Our hearts are *all* we have.

When we lose our hearts, we are not merely making mistakes; we are losing at the only game we will ever have - life.

I had lost my heart. Utterly.

Sitting here alone in an apartment on the Atlantic Seaboard, I admit I don't have the skills to articulate myself well enough so that those who *need* to hear can relate to my story.

I lost my dad long before I could figure out the dissonance between us. Long before I could learn to play the piano well enough. Long before I could discover sonship. Long before he could say: *she* is the one. He is dead now.

I lost my heart on a woman who did not surrender to the same place where - when I finally woke up - I was already spent.

I couldn't pick up the pieces we call life, even when it was required of me.

But now I am past forty. Now I need to man up even though I have no real idea of what it means.

I preach Christ. But I still fall… most days.

I dream of leaving a legacy pointing wholeheartedly to Yahweh. But I drink too much, I fall sexually, I stumble… Incessantly.

I still dream of being a singer-songwriter but most days I still pass unnoticed - tending to other people's dreams that matter more than mine.

Sadly, I lost my inner child, long ago.

I am the peacemaker. The eternal scholar. The hopeful inspirer. But I am also the guy on heart medication. I am the one running alone because I am *not* who I wish I'd be, should others really figure me out.

I sincerely hope that as you read this, you are hearing your own story, not mine. As much as *I* matter, you do. We do. And this is Good News.

Whatever king David's motivation was for pursuing a married woman who was bathing on a roof while *he* was supposed to be out in the fields... Yahweh God invited him back to a responsive heart.

Yahweh gave David a single option: to surrender his own heart back to God - the *only* Strong Authority.

> *"...now unto Him*
> *who is able to keep you from stumbling,*
> *and to set you in the presence of His worth,*
> *unblemished, in gladness,*
> *to God our Saviour, Who alone is wise:*
> *be worth and greatness, power and authority,*
> *both now and to all the ages.*
> *Amen."*
>
> *- Jude 1:24-25*

6

MAMMON

*"I must get my soul back from you;
I am killing my flesh without it."*

- Sylvia Plath

This chapter is numbered six because the number 6 in Hebrew refers to 'man' or 'mankind':

Our ultimate problem.

I left this chapter for last.

Intentionally.

"Today as always, men fall into two groups: *slaves* and *free men*. Whoever does *not* have two-thirds of his day for himself, is a slave, whatever he may be: a statesman, a businessman, an official, or a scholar."
- Friedrich Nietzsche

Interesting how a statement by a man of renown has appeal. But when the Scriptures speak with life-giving advice on freedom, we brush it off as 'spiritual' or 'outdated'. And so, the voice of reason becomes obscured by self-imposed wisdom. Or lack thereof.

Money is a tough one. The concept of having [access to] 'resources' affects us all, regardless of our social standing. Volumes have been written on the subject like George Clason's "Richest Man in Babylon" (1926) and the popular memoir "Rich Dad Poor Dad" (1997) by Robert Kiyosaki.

Since I am innately included in the resource's dilemma, I have no choice but to relay my odyssey with money. This chapter is about the showdown between two gods. On another level it's a story of redemption from slavery.

Our parents were never affluent. They were both successful music teachers, but we were part of the 'middle class' nonetheless - a household with an income above the median. My mother was and still is an extravagant giver - to the point that she'd give away her last penny without overthinking it. As her son and a witness... she often did. But all of this to her credit. No pun intended!

My dad was a little more understated in his spending. His calculated and risk-averse style had a gleam of mystery to it that withstood the test of time. Suffice to say, he was skilled with money.

Teachers earned very little, but I was always pleasantly surprised by all his secret hide-outs and saving schemes. He was elated to reveal some of these secrets at the most random of times. But never in a pompous fashion.

I think back of my dad as a humble and prudent genius when it came to resources. He never had any debt and bought every asset they ever owned in cash.

Myself, on the other hand…

During my High School years, I was a waiter at a local Steak Ranch. I hated every shift but I did enjoy working for my own pocket money. It was stupendously little, but it made up for the slog.

I recall little from the gap year I took after school except that I was *really* poor. But I think my gregarious personality helped me survive somehow.

My parents issued me with a small weekly allowance during my first year at varsity, but I soon realised that even coffee and cake for two would empty my funds. I began sitting "deurwag". This is Afrikaans for a male security guard at a female residence. The shift times were 19:00 to 07:00 at a nominal rate of R12 per hour. I didn't think of *that* as a gateway to a wealth portfolio, but… it sure plugged some holes.

If I am honest with myself, I never had enough money during my varsity years. Yet somehow, I managed to scheme my way into travelling overseas at least once a year. I played gigs, worked as a music director for the student church, sat "deurwag" and did all sorts of things to earn extra cash. But my personality was always slightly in the way. I would easily spend my last penny on pleasures (including people!) simply because I loved it. Looking back now I can spot my ego motivation in most of it. I also recall having had a bit of an expensive taste in just about everything. Except for clothes. My peers and I were a bunch of weirdos who wore mostly outdoor apparel.

My first credit card was… the first dim, red light. I had a minute overdraft facility. But I used it. And I justified it. And in the beginning, it was easy to pay back the debt. But a pattern formed, and *that* was the problem.

KILIMANJARO

In the year 2000, we went to climb Kilimanjaro. Very few of the 16 of us had any money. It cost about R 13,000 per person for a 6-day excursion plus a week-long holiday on Zanzibar. Ridiculously cheap but in those days, it was a lot.

Most of our group members were sponsored by their parents. But my dad offered to lend me the full amount on condition that I pay it back to him at the end of that year.

This sounded perfect to me as it meant I would have another working holiday (read: adventure) in London.

After three stupendous weeks of cutting Christmas trees in the English fields, I recall the sense of bliss when I transferred the full amount I owed my dad.

I was grateful that my parents didn't just give me the money. But I am also aware that something in that Kilimanjaro-London-episode expedited my future consent of borrowing money before I could actually afford it.

My folks sponsored my first four years at varsity. The final two years of my studies I had to pay back. But there was a sense of trust between me and my dad after the successful settlement of my Kili account. My dad wanted me to make more conservative financial choices. But he also recognised something of his own entrepreneurial spirit in me. This contributed to the unsolved mystery between us.

My relationship with money has always been intricately linked to my music, from an early age. I recall several music tours to England and Scotland, and music outreaches to Turkey and Kyrgyzstan. These projects held the promise of riches and unintentionally introduced me to the 'fear and greed' pendulum.

But nothing could prepare me for the money matters that would ensue with our first business: *Merchant Records*. My good friend Daniel and I made heaps of money in our first year. But we were in our early twenties, he was a newlywed and I was just simply living a crazy nomadic life.

We made money before we had the wisdom to steward it well. "You cannot fire a cannon from a canoe." Or more to the point, "When firing a cannon from a canoe, you only have one shot."

In our first business year we saw an opportunity and took it (by the way, in his book "Richest Man in Babylon", Clason defines this as 'luck'), and it worked! But with our lack of experience, we thought our luck translated into a formula for the second year. We signed artists left, right and centre, and spent too much on high-risk ventures. And... we lost everything towards the end of that year. Our luck ran out.

ENTERS DEBT

Daniel and I had little choice but to borrow money from *The Bank* (emphasis added). We had a list of creditors, signed contracts with artists and distributors, high overheads, but above all: a financial vocabulary too limited for mitigating the storm. We were not able to contextualise our problem in terms of *slavery* and how that actually worked, but we were soon to find out.

The blissful exploration of our dreams turned into a nightmare of negotiations, back paddling and sleepless nights. One thing was sure: we needed an intervention.

Our label had begun working with artist and entrepreneur Louis Brittz and a number of promising deals with Christian musicians kept our hopes alive. But three years of Merchant Records finally ended when we gave away the brand.

Daniel and I parted ways. He and his wife left for Europe and I remained in Stellenbosch. Miracle upon miracle, I managed to claw my way out of the most immediate threats: bank loans, creditors and the South African Revenue Service.

I began my solo music production path in 2005 with almost a quarter-million Rands of personal debt. This is *not* the most advisable way to launch anything. The road to recovery - at least from my perspective - started with a decade long journey of discovery. But I was so steeped in debt at the time that I did not have the capacity to face my *actual* dilemma.

My friend Hannes and I undertook a three-week backpacking trip to Zambia and Malawi. I needed the emotional renegade to gain some clarity after our failed business. I actually *borrowed* money from a friend in the music industry for my travels. We experienced the raw freedom and beauty of thousands of kilometres of open roads through Southern Africa… but on a heart level, I felt trapped to the core. I recall my anguish as I thought back on what felt like a three-year ambush.

After Merchant Records I worked as a part-time lecturer at the Conservatorium and recorded lists of albums for local acts. The University allowed me to hire their studios at a rate which seemed fair, but my curious love for numbers soon made me realise that there could be another option.

My naive view on what freedom from slavery meant pushed me to max out two credit cards to buy my own studio equipment! I did *not* recover from this for years, but deep down, I was becoming entangled with debt in a way that felt beautiful. And justifiable.

My mind was darkened.

This pattern continued for years. I would make money, appease my credit cards, and make more debt. And as much as I *wanted* this cycle to stop, I couldn't. There was something so messed up in my perception of work, money and feeling trapped that I justified *all* forms of spending just to escape it. And my only backup plan was more credit facilities. I had no savings for retirement, no annuity, no investments, no shares, no nothing! I simply believed the lie that the best investment was in my own set of skills to produce music - aka 'generate money'.

I was trapped.

I've always owned expensive cars, which not only made me feel better about my life but also boosted my public profile that I justified as part of marketing myself.

Robert Kiyosaki in his book "Rich Dad Poor Dad" speaks about the two emotional drivers behind money: *fear* and *greed*.

When we have access to too much, greed kicks in. When we have access to too little, fear takes over. Sometimes it is even the other way around. Whichever way, for most people, most of the time, the sway of the pendulum is continuous.

Once this becomes a pattern, we arrive full circle back at Nietzsche's *slaves* and *free men*.

I know that the idea of 'slaves' and 'free men' is more complex than I am framing it. Many people who have lots in the bank and own many assets are still slaves. And many who own very little are completely free. The conversation about freedom has nothing to do with beating the financial system. It's a God conversation. And since it's the focal point, I need to emphasise that our finances are a heart-thing. And a treasure-thing.

> *"...where your treasure is,*
> *there your heart shall also be."*
> *- Yeshua (Matthew 6:21)*

That which we ultimately value points to our ultimate allegiance. In religious terms, our treasures always point to what or who we worship.

Slavery and freedom are not merely demarcated by money or lack thereof. At the end of the day, it is about what or who we trust. In most cases - and sadly the followers of Christ are *not* indemnified against it - our trust is in something or someone other than God.

Therefore, I believe that the relationship we have with resources essentially highlights the status of our hearts. That is why we can only either surrender unto Mammon or God. Any attempt at fidelity to both will mean using the one to pay or bribe the other. Sadly, this is the way that many believers handle the difficult subject of *tithing:* pay God in the hope that He will eventually give me more money.

When we left for the *Shmitah* in 2014, I had about R120k of credit card debt. And we were about to embark on a two-year sabbatical from working for money.

I justified this reckless position because Emile and I were yoked together, and there was the initial understanding that we would share the load.

In June 2014 during our short visit to South Africa, a friend of mine sat me down one day and asked me directly, "Helmut, are you in debt?" I had nothing left but my frail ego, so I revealed to her the extent of my financial plight.

At the time my total credit card debt huddled around R140k. I also still owned my Land Rover Freelander which cost me a fortune per month. The humiliation of that moment was greater than my actual financial predicament.

My friend then requested that I take out all my credit cards and cut them in pieces, right there and then. She then opened her laptop and transferred almost the full amount outstanding to my credit cards.

"I am taking your debt on me. Because I believe in your mission. Please go and make no debt again."

That moment changed everything.

I sold one or two last pieces of studio gear and settled all my debt. One of our team member's family needed an SUV, and they took over my Freelander's payments. I arrived back in Israel in July debt-free and with some money in the bank. From that moment onwards it *never* ran out.

The same year while on a train ride in London I had the sudden thought of opening three separate bank accounts: one for giving away, one for tax and one for savings. Strangest thought ever as I was without income and definitely not tuned in to channelling resources.

I went onto my banking app and set up these accounts. I then understood with almost surreal clarity that 10% of all my income needed to go to each of these accounts. That would mean living on 70% of all future income. Again… an unusual thought.

That same day somebody anonymously paid R100 into my bank account. And just as the inner voice prompted, I moved R10 to each of the three new accounts and understood that R70 was for spending. This system is in place to this day.

Following the *Shmitah* and Jubilee years, I returned to normal work life and kept this pattern to the tee with a deep awareness that the still small voice that day in London was the voice of God.

BITCOIN

I was part of the 2017 Bitcoin (BTC) rush when most people lost a lot of money in the 'big crash'. It remained a bit of a nebulous topic. Nonetheless, I had R16,000 worth of BTC in an exchange wallet, and decided to join a BTC trading platform.

I have to admit that during that first month, I did experience a surge of hope that the BTC investment might help me in some way, but I was utterly unprepared for what lay ahead.

By mid-December 2019, the growth of my BTC portfolio matched my expenses for the month! I could not believe what was happening to me. Typically, Decembers would bring more stress and debt than any other month. But for the first time I could remember, my month was paid for in full.

I recall lying on the floor of my mother's retirement abode - the words of my doctor ringing in my ears: "Helmut, you will have to find another way to make a living."

SWITZERLAND

January 2020 was the first of its kind for me. I drove from Cape Town all the way to Pretoria to record four singles for a client of ours. *That* was my first experience of making music without the pressure of selling my time.

In February I left Cape Town for Zurich for a month-long working holiday in Switzerland. I was booked to record Anne-Marie van Eeden's album from her home by Lake Geneva, followed by a 10-day writing stint, and then another 5-track EP for our mutual friend Fransien Scott.

Anne-Marie and I finished most of our recordings for her 8-track album "Verhaal" by the time I left Montreux. I rented a VW in Geneva and headed for the mystical alpine village of Zermatt.

I was determined to sit in my hostel lounge - overlooking the insanely mesmerising *Matterhorn* - and write for five days! But as life pans out for 7's on the Enneagram, my German roommate Ulrich convinced me to join him in climbing the *Breithorn*.

Now the Breithorn, kissing the skyline at 4164 meters, is known to be the easiest accessible alpine peak above 4000 meters. Not so much so. Especially not for climbers without crampons and ice axes.

Nonetheless, off we went. We took the ski lift from Zermatt to Klein Matterhorn (3800m), where the outside temperature was around minus 12. Stepping out onto the ice, I felt dizzy and nervous about how my heart would act under the circumstances.

I had enough water, snacks and some emergency goods. But as we headed out onto the glacier, I could sense that my body was definitely *not* groomed for these conditions.

We started our cautious ascend up the steep ice slope, determined to reach the summit in about three hours. But as we passed the halfway mark, the mist cleared, and the day turned into a bright and sunny affair. The only problem was that the heat started melting the snow, which then immediately froze into ice. By the time we realised this, we were already *in* trouble. Every step we took was less secure than the one before, but we managed to reach a rocky slope which provided some solid footing for most of the ridge leading to the summit.

I wish I could show a picture of what we faced as we reached the summit. The entire slope had turned to ice. And we had *nothing* to mitigate the imminent catastrophe. We started crawling and dragging our frozen bodies up the ice ledge with a blizzard in our faces so that we could barely hear each other scream. I prayed non-stop for mercy. I don't know how we made it to the top. But I was trounced with fear.

And then the unimaginable happened. When I could finally get to my feet for the first time in more than an hour of crawling, I stepped into a small ice crack and probably due to the freezing cold, tore the ligaments of my right ankle. I fell down and wanted to vomit of pain and dizziness. But we needed to get down another ice slope. One ankle out of action.

I experienced how the hand of God carried me down that day. At times I couldn't see Ulrich as the ice and mist blurred our vision and I fell and slid more than once for what felt like meters. But I just clung to the hope of a second chance. And faced the utter stupidity of our decision to climb the Breithorn.

The miracle of reaching Zermatt safely became a metaphor for the rest of 2020.

ENTERS COVID

The rest of my month in Switzerland I continued with my ankle brace – frustrated, to say the least – but visited some of the most picturesque landmarks in the country: Lauterbrunnen, the Jungfrau, the quaint villages of Isenfluh, Grindelwald and several more.

My entire Swiss holiday was made possible by a constantly growing crypto investment. I wrapped up the month of music-making and departed with a sense of restoration.

I spent my last few days in Montreux strolling along Lake Geneva and keeping an eye on the news from abroad - word about a 'deadly virus' spreading uncontrollably from China started popping up everywhere.

By the time I got to Zurich Airport for my return flight, it seemed that the world had transformed into a badly designed movie set. The airport was almost deserted. Rows of check-in counters were closed. The few people who *did* fly wore masks and had 'fear' written all over them. Even at Cape Town International, the sudden reaction to this global threat was palpable.

I stayed with my mother in her retirement home for a couple of days, but the community of elderly people did *not* appreciate me arriving from Europe and hanging out with them in close proximity. My COVID test came back negative. But I was no longer welcome in the retirement village…

Together with my friends Jandre and Werner, we recorded a minimalistic 11-track album in six days, just prior to Christmas 2019. We hid out in an old farmhouse in the Ceres Karoo, with no mobile reception, and simply made some of the best music I was ever part of. Our rules were simple: quick and intuitive musical decisions, lots of good wine, nightly barbecues and a week of Karoo skies and hanging out as friends.

We launched the album in the same house where we recorded. We played the album from top to bottom through studio monitors and to a small crowd of about fifty. It made for a fresh event. That same evening, I met the owner of a farmhouse with an adjacent studio situated in the mountains of Tulbagh. Two weeks later, South Africa went into a three-week *lockdown*. Since I had no place to live, I was quite pleased that I saved his number. "Jannie! Helmut here. We met two weeks ago at *that* CD launch outside Ceres…"

He remembered me.

UNTETHERED

"Umm. About that farmhouse with the studio…" And that was the start of five indescribable months at *Fisaasbos*, nestled high up in the charming horseshoe where the Witzenberg valley touches the Klein Winterhoek Mountains.

A friend joined me, and we lived secluded from the outside world. Our days were marked by wellness. We both wrote books and crisscrossed the mountains we had all to ourselves! I went for a solo run one afternoon, and a still small voice broke the silence of the forest:

"If you will keep what I am entrusting to you to yourself, it will be short-lived. But if you give according to how I prompt you, there shall be no end to this."

These were the words I felt almost audibly in my heart.

I sat down with my friend after that experience and decided to launch an initiative to help a list of people. As I look back on this road of discovering the dynamics of giving away resources *obediently*, I'm startled.

Truthfully, I can't employ the word 'obedient' as if I've got this figured out. I don't. But I *am* learning, and I am seeing fruit beyond what I could imagine.

GOD AND MAMMON

The word "MAMMON" came into English from the Latin *mammona,* meaning 'wealth', but was borrowed from the Hellenistic Greek ("MAMMON"), which appears in the New Testament, in turn borrowed from the Aramaic ("MAMONA"). Evidence points to the Syriac dialect, with *mamona* meaning 'wealth' or 'profit', but if we trace the origins and uses of this word throughout Mishnaic Hebrew and its uses within Canaanite context, it [may] simply mean: 'that in which one trusts'.

Hebrew makes a distinction between 'wealth' and 'riches'. And even though we're in the domain of semantics here, I need to point out that the word for 'wealth' is "CHAYIL". This word literally means 'power' or 'force' and could be related to either an army or resources. It should be obvious that it does *not* by any means have an evil connotation.

The Hebrew word for 'riches' is "OSHER". This noun is rooted in the verb "ASHAR" which means 'to accumulate' or 'to grow'. Again, nothing evil here. Our interpretation hinges on how we hold this paradox.

My dear friend Michael Hack, who has mentored me through my ignorant and reckless years, introduced me to the following principle:

"The world is all about buying and selling; the Kingdom, in contrast, is all about giving and receiving."

This may be the crux: when we discover the power of giving away that which we value, whilst simultaneously becoming open to receiving what we need, we are beginning to discover the deceitfulness of *Mammon*.

Mammon is all about control. And control is all about that which we fear and that which we desire. If we only honour the principle of buying and selling, I am afraid that we have yielded at least some power - and therefore authority - to something or someone other than God.

I discovered freedom when I discovered the power of giving money away. And all the more so giving away that which I received freely. I am *not* saying we should not have wealth. I am advocating for the exact opposite! But under the condition that we learn to receive and give away.

Over the past months, I have witnessed how the mystery of God trumps the fascism that Yeshua refers to as 'Mammon'.

Maybe this is what Yeshua refers to in his parable in Luke 16. The way we deal with unrighteous Mammon may just be an indication of how we will handle *that* which is far more important to God: people, His treasure.

To be sure, I am still learning.

To Yahweh alone belongs all the glory, all the wealth, all the power, and *all* the allegiance.

Now, and forever.

12

EPILOGUE

"Habit, not hope, is the last thing to go."

- Pedro Cabiya

"MACH'SHEV" is the Modern Hebrew word for 'computer' and is derived from the verbal root form "CHASHAV", meaning 'to think'.

When a "MEM" is prefixed to this verb, the noun "MACH'SHEV" is formed, concretely meaning 'what thinks' - a computer.

Both these words also occur in Ancient Hebrew, but with a slight aberration.

PATTERNS

"YHWH saw that the wickedness of man was great in the earth, and that every imagination of the thoughts of his heart was only evil continually."
- Genesis 6:5 (WEB)

In respect for the eminence of hermeneutics, I need to state categorically that this verse - specifically nestled into the controversial arena of the *Nephilim* or 'giants of old' - cannot be read out of context. In short: the text hints to the pervasive presence of a group of fallen, demi-human beings called "HA'NEPHILIM", literally meaning 'the fallen ones'. And we know the illustrious story of angels mingling with humans.

With His intention to destroy the world through a flood, God instructed Noah - the hero of the Genesis 6 narrative - to build an ark. And as motivation for this - textual ambiguity taken into account - Genesis 6:5 is under the spotlight.

Firstly, the phrases "...*wickedness* of man..." and "...was only *evil*..." are related concepts, as they share the common adjective "RA", literally meaning 'to leave the path'. Our Western minds perceive the concept of 'being evil' through a philosophical and moral lens; for the Ancients it merely meant straying from a prescribed path or trail.

Secondly, the translated phrase "...every imagination of the thoughts of his heart..." is possibly one of the strongest Hebrew expressions we may find in the text. Transliterated, it reads:

"...V'KOL YETSER MACH'SHAVOT LIVO..."

Literally: "...and every purpose of the patterns of his heart..." and then it proceeds with another strong statement:

"...RAQ RA' KOL-HAYOM."

Translated as "...is only leaving the path, every day." When we put this together:

"YHWH saw that mankind's straying from the path *is* great on earth. And every intention of the *habits* of his heart is only leaving the path. Always." I have added punctuation and emphasis for ease of reading, but very little explanation for this statement is needed.

The Biblical Hebrew word behind 'habit' is "MACH'SHAV". This word literally means 'a weaving' as in following a strict pattern of interlacing to weave a blanket, carpet or any piece of fabric. The respective ancient and modern uses of this word are etymologically linked through the idea of an *algorithm*.

The late Derek Prince stated, "Your character is the sum total of your habits."

Without attempting to make a value statement concerning identity, we can conclude we *are* what we repeatedly do.

FRACTAL

Seventeen months since I penned down the prologue to this volume, I now begin to understand the beauty and the dilemma of the patterns we live by and the habits we form - many of which are the results of circumstances or relationships beyond our control. From many of these we need rescue. And rescue is most often actuated by some sort of intervention.

My own awareness was triggered by three heart procedures; yours may be a totally different path.

But at the end of the day, we are the complex tapestries of patterns and habits, living with a singular hope that "all things work together for good for those who love Elohim and are called according to *His* purpose." (Romans 8:28)

GLOSSARY

The following Hebrew words are used in this volume, indexed according to Strong's numbering.

Each first occurrence in Scripture is referenced.
Abbreviations used:
adv - adverb
adj - adjective
f - feminine
m - masculine
n - noun
p - plural
s - singular
v - verb
c - construct state (designating possession between two nouns)

H121 (s,m,n) **ADAM** (אדם) - "Red". Name of the first man, derived from "ADAMAH" (H127 / אדמה) - as in 'from the ground' - and sharing the exact same spelling as H120 meaning 'mankind'. Genesis 2:19

H127 (s,f,n) **ADAMAH** (אדמה) - "Ground" or "Soil". Genesis 1:25

H376 (s,m,n) **ISH** (אִישׁ) - "Man". Referring to an individual male person. This noun is derived from the noun "ENOSH" (H582 / אֱנוֹשׁ), meaning 'a mortal'. Furthermore, the noun "ENOSH" is derived from the verbal form "ANASH" (H605 / אנשׁ), literally meaning 'to be weak' or 'to be frail'. Genesis 2:23

H430 (p,m,n) **ELOHIM** (אלהים) - "God" or "gods". Plural form of the word "EL" (H410 / אל). Picture of an ox and a shepherd's staff. Literal meaning: 'strong authority'. Genesis 1:1

H571 (s,f,n) **EMET** (אמת) - "Truth". This could also be understood to mean 'stability'. Picture of an ox, water and a marker. Literal meaning: 'glue of the covenant'. Genesis 24:27

H802 (s,f,n) **ISHAH** (אִשָּׁה) - "Woman" or "Wife". "ISHAH" is the feminine form of the masculine noun "ISH" (H376 / אִישׁ). In Ancient understanding, a boy only transitioned into manhood when he was coupled with [his] "ISHAH". Genesis 2:22

H875 (s,f,n) **BE'ER** (באר) - "Well" or "Pit". Derived from the verb "BA'AR" (H874 / באר) which means 'to dig'. Genesis 14:10

H905 (s,m,n) **L'VADO** (לבדו) - "For him to be alone". The root form here is the word "BAD" meaning 'by itself'. Genesis 2:18

H1254 (s,m,v) **BARA** (ברא) - "He created". When context across the various uses within the Hebrew text is considered, a better translation would be 'to fashion' or 'to fill'. Genesis 1:1

H1320 (s,m,n) **BASAR** (בשר) - "Flesh". Rooted in the verbal form with the same spelling, meaning 'to be full' or 'fresh'. 1 Samuel 4:17

H1683 (s,f,n) **DEVORAH** (דבֹרה) - "Bee". A village in modern Israel and the name of two Israelite women. Same as H1682 referencing the orderly motion of a bee. Genesis 35:8

H1893 (s,m,n) **HEVEL** (הבל) - "Breath". Abel (Hevel) was the second son of Adam and Eve, killed by his brother Cain ("Qayin"). Genesis 4:2

H1961 (p,f,v) **HEYOT** (היוֹת) - "To be". Conjugated from the singular verb "HAYAH", meaning 'to exist' or 'to become'. Genesis 1:2

H1984 (s,m,v) **HALAL** (הלל) - "To be clear" (as in 'sounding') or "to shine" (as in 'being bright'). This verb is usually translated as 'to praise', but literally refers to the observation - even fixation upon - something or someone. A more functional translation would be 'to fix [your] eyesight on...' Genesis 12:15

H2145 (s,m,n) **ZAKAR** (זכר) - "Male". This Hebrew noun is derived from the verbal form with the same spelling (H2142), meaning 'to remember' or 'call to mind'. This grounds the concept of being male as 'one that remembers'. Genesis 1:27

H2332 (s,f,n) **CHAVAH** (חוה) - "Eve". The Hebrew word behind the English name 'Eve' literally means 'life-giver'. Genesis 3:20

H2416 (s,f,adj) **CHAYAH** (ח'ה) - "Living" or "Alive". Rooted in the verbal form with the same spelling, meaning 'to have life'. Genesis 1:20

H2428 (s,m,n) **CHAYIL** (ח'ל) - "Strength" or "Might". This word is very often translated as 'wealth', but specifically in the sense of 'ability' or 'force', whether of men or other resources. Genesis 34:29

H2889 (s,m,v) **TAHOR** (טהור) - "Clean" or "Pure". Best understood as 'ceremonially undefiled'. Derived from the verbal form "TAHER" (H2891 / טהר), meaning 'to be bright'. Genesis 7:2

H2896 (adj) **TOV** (טוֹב) - "Good" or "Agreeable". From a concrete perspective, this adjective is best understood to mean 'functional' as in something that works efficiently or correctly. Genesis 1:4

H3068 (s,m,n) **YHWH** (יהוה) - "Yahweh". This Hebrew word represents the four-letter name of God, called the Tetragrammaton and is traditionally pronounced as 'Jehovah' or 'Yahweh', depending on the school of thought. Rooted in the verbal form "HAYAH" (H1961/ ה'ה), this Hebrew name is best translated as 'He exists' or 'He exists because He has breath'. Genesis 2:4

H3104 (s,m,n) **YOVEL** (יובל) - "Jubilee". This word literally means 'blast of a horn' in reference to the marking of the Year of Jubilee (every 50th year) by the blowing of cornets. It is rooted in the verbal form "YAVAL" (H2986/יבל) meaning 'to flow' or 'to conduct'. Exodus 19:13

H3117 (s,m,n) **YOM** (יום) - "Day" or "Daylight". This word literally means 'hot' or 'from sunrise to sunset' - the part of a 24-hour cycle during which the sun shines. In Scripture it usually designates one complete day. Genesis 1:5

H3336 (s,m,n) **YETSER** (יצר) - "A form" or "Framework". Derived from the verbal root "YATSAR" (H3335/יצר) meaning 'to form' or 'to frame' with intention. Genesis 6:5

H3442 (s,m,n) **YESHUA** (יֵשׁוּעַ) - "Jesus". The English name 'Jesus' was transliterated first from the Hebrew word 'Yeshua' to the Greek word 'Iesous' (Χριστός), and from there to the English name 'Jesus'. The Hebrew name 'Yeshua' is an Aramaic shorthand variant of the longer Hebrew word "YEHOSHUA" (H3091/יְהוֹשֻׁעַ), better known as 'Joshua'. This Hebrew name means 'Yahweh is salvation' or 'Yahweh saves'. In the Hebrew text, the word 'Yeshua' references two Iraelites as well as a geographical location. 1 Chronicles 24:11

H3478 (s,m,n) **YISRA'EL** (ישראל) - "Israel". The name 'Israel' is a composite between the verb "SARAH" (H8280/שרה), which means 'to prevail' or 'to have power', and the Hebrew word "EL" (H410/אל) - the shorthand for the word "ELOHIM". Put together, this two word comprise "YISRA'EL", meaning 'Elohim prevails'. Genesis 32:28

H3612 (s,m,n) **CALEV** (כלב) - "Kaleb". One of the courageous and faithful spies who reported favourably on the Promised Land. Also literally 'a dog' - due to the possible construct of the words "KOL" (H3605/כָּל) - meaning 'every' or 'all' - and "LEV", meaning 'heart'. Numbers 13:6

H3667 (s,m,n) **KENA'AN** (כנען) - "Canaan". Literally: 'lowland' or 'land below'. Rooted in the verb "KANA" (H3665/כנע) which means 'to be humble' or 'to bend the knee'. Genesis 9:18

H3725 (pl,m,n) **HAKIPPURIM** (הַכִּפֻּרִים) - "The Coverings". This word is traditionally translated as 'Atonement' and is commonly known as 'The Day of Atonement' when in conjunction with "YOM". The root word "KIPPUR" is derived from the verbal form "KAPHAR" (H3722/כפר) which means 'to cover'. Exodus 29:36

H3808 (adv) **LO** (לא) - "Not". By implication meaning 'no'. Genesis 2:5

H3820 (s,m,n) **LEV** (לב) - "The heart". Picture of a shepherd's staff and a tent. Literal meaning: 'authority within'. Genesis 6:5

H4284 (pl,f,n) **MACH'SHAVOT** (מחשבת) - "Contrivances". Best explained as 'patterns' and derived from the verbal root form "CHASHAV" (H2803/חשב) meaning 'to plait', 'to weave' or 'to fabricate'. Genesis 6:5

H4317 (s,m,n) **MICHAEL** (מיכאל) - "Who is like God". The Arch Angel. The feminine version of "MICHAEL" is "MICHAELA" and has the same meaning. It is constructed of three Hebrew words: "MI" (H4310/מי) - meaning 'who is'; "KI" (H3588/כי) - meaning 'like' and "EL" (H410/אל) - meaning 'Elohim'. Numbers 13:13

H5048 (s,m,adv) **K'NEGDO** (כנגדו) - "Like his counterpart". This conjugated adjective is rooted in the verbal form "NAGAD" (H5046/נגד), which literally means 'to boldly stand out opposite'. This verb can also be understood as 'to announce', 'to certify' or 'to declare' - but always in the concrete sense of fronting another person or, figuratively, confronting a situation. Genesis 2:18

H5303 (pl,m,n) **HA'NEPHILIM** (הנפלים) - "The fallen". Derived from the verbal root "NAPHAL" (H5307/נפל), meaning 'to fall' or 'to be cast down'. Often translated as 'the giants'. Genesis 6:4

H5315 (s,f,n) **NEPHESH** (נפש) - "A complete being". Most often translated as 'soul', but literally meaning 'a breathing creature'. Genesis 1:20

H5347 (s,f,n) **NEQEVAH** (נקבה) - "Female". This noun is derived from the verbal form "NAQAV" (H5344/נקב) literally meaning 'to puncture' or 'to pierce'. The word "NEQEVAH" literally means 'one that is pierced' (in a sexual sense), but figuratively, the 'pierced one' is understood as the one that sets or designates [the] boundaries. Genesis 1:27

H5523 (pl,f,n) **SUKKOT** (סֻכֹּת) - "Booths". The name of the first place the Israelites stopped when they left Egypt. Also the name of a feast traditionally known as 'The Feast of Tabernacles'. Derived from both the singular feminine noun "SUKKAH" (H5521/סכה) - meaning 'a temporary shelter - as well the masculine noun "SOK" (H5520/סך) meaning 'a hut made of entwined boughs'. Genesis 33:17

H5680 (adj) **IVRI** (עברי) - "Hebrew". Literally translated: 'one from beyond'. This Hebrew adjective is derived from the noun "EVER" (H5677/עבר) - 'the region beyond' - in turn derived from the verb "AVAR" (H5674/עבר) which means 'to cross over' or 'make a transition'. Genesis 14:13

H5828 (s,m,n) **EZER** (עזר) - "Help" or "Aid". This could also be interpreted as 'one who helps'. Genesis 2:18

H6175 (adj) **ARUM** (ערום) - "Cunning" or "Shrewd". This adjective is derived from its verbal form "ARAM" (H6191/ערם) meaning 'to be bare' or 'to be shrewd'. Genesis 3:1

H6239 (s,m,n) **OSHER** (עשר) - "Wealth" or "Riches". Rooted in the verbal form "ASHAR" (H6238/עשר) which properly means 'to accumulate'. Genesis 31:16

H6664 (s,m,n) **TSEDEK** (צדק) - "Righteousness". Picture of a trail, a door and the horizon (as in the place where light gathers). Literal meaning: 'a path leading to the entrance of a gathering'. Leviticus 19:15

H7014 (s,m,n) **QAYIN** (קין) - "Possession". Eldest son of Adam and Eve and murderer of his brother Abel (Hevel). The name 'Cain' is related to the Hebrew word "QAYIN" (H7013/קין) meaning a 'lance' or 'spear'. Genesis 4:1

H7307 (s,f,n) **RU'ACH** (רוח) - "Breath" or "Wind". Most Western translations employ the word 'spirit' whenever the context is sufficiently abstract. Genesis 1:2

H7451 (adj) **RA** (רע) - "Evil". Picture of a man and an eye. Possible translation could be 'man searching out other possibilities'. The Ancients understood the concept of "RA" as straying from a trusted or prescribed path. Genesis 2:9

H7535 (adv) **RAQ** (רק) - "Only". Literally meaning 'leanness' as in a limitation. Genesis 6:5

H7585 (s,f,n) **SHE'OL** (שאול) - "Underworld". Sometimes translated as 'the grave', "SHE'OL" refers to place the Hebrews were uncertain of its whereabouts. It is derived from the verbal root "SHA'AL" (H7592/שאל), meaning 'to ask where it is'. Genesis 37:35

H7651 (s,m,n) **SHEVA** (שבע) - The cardinal number "Seven". Derived from the root verb "SHAVA" (H7650/שבע) which literally means 'to swear' or 'to be complete'. The odd relation between these two meanings is the seven repetitions of a declaration needed to seal or make an oath. Literally: 'to seven oneself'. Genesis 4:24

H7676 (s,f,n) **SHABBAT** (שבת) - "Sabbath". The only day of the week with a designated name, in contrast with the other six days of the week. The word "SHABBAT" literally means 'a cessation' and is derived from the verb "SHAVAT" (H7673/שבת) meaning 'to cease', 'to desist' or 'to repose' from exertion or labour. Exodus 16:23

H7812 (s,m,v) **SHACHAH** (שחה) - "Bow down". The act of bowing prostrate before somebody in respect to their perceived value. This verb is usually translated as 'to worship' when used in conjunction with man unto God, and as 'to do obeisance' when used in conjunction with man unto man. A more literal translation, based on the pictographic letters, is 'to remove the barrier of the eyesight.' We therefore conclude that the action of bowing down in respect to another, amends the perceived value of the other person or being. Genesis 18:2

H8057 (s,f,n) **SIMCHAH** (שמחה) - "Joy". Derived from the adjective "SAME'ACH" (H8056/שמח) - meaning 'joyful' or 'merry' - which in turn is derived from the verb

"SAMACH" (H8055/שמח), meaning 'to rejoice' or 'to be glad'. Genesis 31:27

H8059 (s,f,n) **SHMITAH** (שמטה) - "Remission". This Hebrew noun is the name of the seventh year, also known as the 'year of release'. Seven cycles of seven years, each ending with a "SHMITAH", is followed by a 50th 'Year of Jubilee' ("HA'YOBEL). The word "SHMITAH" is rooted in the verbal form "SHAMAT" (H8058/שמט), meaning 'to release' or 'to let alone'. Deuteronomy 15:1

H8141 (pl,f,n,c) **SH'NAT** (שנת) - "Year of…" The simple form is "SHANEH" and is derived from the root verb "SHANAH" (H8138/שנה) meaning 'to duplicate' or 'repeat'. Genesis 1:14

H8643 (s,f,n) **TERU'AH** (תרועה) - "A Sounding". This could be the sounding of an alarm, a shout, a blast or clamour of any kind. When used in conjunction with the word "YOM", we have the name of a festival known in the Scriptures as 'The Feast of Trumpets' - or literally: 'day of sounding'. The verbal root "RUWA" (H7321/רוע) means 'to sound', 'to mar' or figuratively 'to split the ears'. Leviticus 23:24

ACKNOWLEDGEMENTS

I want to express deep gratitude towards the names mentioned in this volume for the roles they played in my account. Several individuals however are not mentioned; I want to single out Rudolph du Toit, Ferdinand Dick, Ian Pollard, Konstand Spies and Sven Blumer. You are first and foremost companions without whom the journey would be nought.

Thank you, Marcelle Balt, for editing this body of work. There was not a shortage of editors but considering the depth of our shared journey and your prowess, there was only one. Melani Jacobs - thank you for an incredible cover design. You got the essence, instantly.

To my mentors and sages, I would be nowhere without amongst others: Michael Hack, Theo Geyser, Skip Moen, Jeff Benner… thank you. To my mother, sister and late father: you remain central to my motivation.

And finally, to my Master, the King of Israel and eternal mystery of YHWH: Yeshua Messiah - all I am, for all You are!

This offering is for You.

ABOUT THE AUTHOR

Helmut Meijer is an award-winning, South African music producer, composer, singer-songwriter as well as a scholar and teacher of the Ancient Hebrew language.

He holds a degree in Science (Zoology and Geography), as well as a Master of Philosophy degree in Music Technology (cum laude) at the University of Stellenbosch, South Africa.

Helmut regularly travels to and leads non-commercial tours to Israel and enjoys spending time in the outdoors.

www.ingramcontent.com/pod-product-compliance
Lightning Source LLC
LaVergne TN
LVHW020927090426
835512LV00020B/3252